The Treatment of Shame and Guilt in Alcoholism Counseling

ABOUT THE EDITORS

Ronald T. Potter-Efron, MSW, PhD, is a clinical psychotherapist for Midelfort Clinic in Eau Claire, Wisconsin.

Patricia S. Potter-Efron is a certified alcoholism counselor in private practice in Eau Claire and a consultant to hospitals that have chemical dependency programs.

The Potter-Efrons hold workshops around the country on such topics as the treatment of shame and guilt in alcoholics and on adult children of alcoholics. They have published articles on family violence and chemical dependency. A primary aspect of their work is the incorporation of Gestalt therapy.

The Treatment of Shame and Guilt in Alcoholism Counseling

Ronald T. Potter-Efron
Patricia S. Potter-Efron
Editors

The Haworth Press
New York • London

The Treatment of Shame and Guilt in Alcoholism Counseling has also been published as *Alcoholism Treatment Quarterly*, Volume 4, Number 2, Summer 1987.

The Haworth Press, Inc., 10 Alice Street, Binghamton, NY 13904–1580
EUROSPAN/Haworth, 3 Henrietta Street, London WC2E 8LU England

Library of Congress Cataloging-in-Publication Data

The Treatment of shame and guilt in alcoholism counseling.

"Has also been published as Alcoholism treatment quarterly, volume 4, number 2, summer 1987" — T.p. verso.
Includes bibliographies.
1. Alcoholics — Mental health. 2. Shame. 3. Guilt. 4. Children of alcoholics — Mental health. 5. Psychotherapy. I. Potter-Efron, Ronald T. II. Potter-Efron, Patricia S. [DNLM: 1. Alcoholism — therapy. 2. Counseling — methods. 3. Family. 4. Guilt. 5. Parent-Child Relations. W1 AL3147 v.4 no.2 / WM 274 T786]
RC565.T75   1988   616.86'1   87-29724
ISBN 0-86656-718-6
ISBN 0-86656-941-3 (pbk.)

The Treatment of Shame and Guilt in Alcoholism Counseling

CONTENTS

The Treatment
of Shame and Guilt
in Alcoholism
Counseling

Shame in the Eighties

Ernest Kurtz, PhD

Because shame is a timeless reality within human experience, attention to it is always seasonable. Yet the sources of that timeliness differ.

Shame's timelessness derives from its revelation of human both-and-ness. We are never all that we think we should be or even might be. But our striving for either-or, our demands for all-or-nothing, founder on the reality of our selves — selves that are "less than the gods, more than the beasts, yet somehow also both." Word-origins hint Shame's relationship to sexuality: it is our intimate vulnerability that makes us who we are,[1]

Understanding the current revival of interest in shame is aided by acknowledging a parallel phenomenon — the equally recent rediscovery of story. Shame and story both have to do with wholeness. Shame's affect arises from, indeed *is*, the feeling that our wholeness is somehow unwhole, that our very being is somehow broken. As several of the articles that follow attest, story in any form reconciles to what wholeness is available.[2]

But a more profound timeliness underlies our era's attention to both shame and story. The 1980s' rediscovery of shame flows from more than mere happenstance. Although shame's modern bibliography begins in the 1950s with the studies of Piers and Singer and the investigations of Helen Merrell Lynd, only in the late seventies and early eighties do popular phenomena reveal the significance of that rediscovery and its specific shaping.[3] It is not accidental that this special volume on shame appears in a journal dedicated to the topic of alcoholism treatment. As thinkers as diverse as John Mack and Christopher Lasch have recently reminded, a narcissistic age craves the spiritual: and the relationships of the spiritual to "spirits" is all too familiar.' Shame's relationship to "the spiritual" will furnish one of our themes.

The articles that follow shed light directly on shame and shame's healing. But they also illuminate the culture within which both occur. Themselves timely, these pieces examine topics as diverse as theories of forgiving and techniques of videotaping, modes of measuring the unquantifiable and methods of enabling storytelling with stuffed animals and modeling clay. Yet deeper thematic unities underlie their placement here together. Both the nature of the phenomenon of shame and the realities of the time at which these studies appear mean that they are both immersed in and reflective of six themes that frame current understandings of shame. Although each paper will not manifest all of these themes. This volume will best serve readers who remain mindful of the sensitivities that unite the contributions' vision. Those sensitivities may be summarized under six brief headings.

THE PERSONAL AND THE PROFESSIONAL

In an era when those involved in the healing of chronic disabilities recognize that technical competence in the modalities of therapy must be complemented by sensitivity to the specifically human dimension of hurt, distinguishing between shame and guilt and attending to shame's specific pain both serves that recognition and enhances healing abilities. For if there be one overriding albeit implicit theme in each of these articles as well as in all the literature on shame, it is that one's personal experience of one's self cannot be separated from one's professional approach to the phenomenon of shame.

Guilt concerns doing, and what we do professionally and personally can be held separate. But shame has to do with *being*, and what we are personally and professionally necessarily touch. Here as rarely elsewhere in professional endeavor, only one who has experienced shame is capable of touching and healing shame. It seems, indeed, that only by understanding shame in one's own life does one become able to accurately identify its impact in another's. How to reconcile this awareness with the valid requirements of professionalism remains an ongoing challenge.

SENSE OF FAILURE, LACK, FLAW

The core of shame consists in the experience of failure — the sense that one is somehow flawed, defective, lacking. Ultimately, shame is an experience of nothingness — the experiencing, however veiled, of one's own nonbeing. One becomes more fully human by and in the processing of that experience. But that process does not necessarily occur. Shame is so painful, our defect of being can feel so hollow, that one may become mired in its misery. There is no disablement more profound than the inability to be human — to *be* humanly — that afflicts a person locked in shame.

Because the demand for all-or-nothing signals the attempt to be other than human, the sufferer becomes locked in shame not by the acknowledgment of flaw but by its denial. An age addicted to "pride," a context in which only "number one" matters, sets up its participants for disablement by shame.

DENIAL — SELF-DECEPTION

For as commentators so regularly note, *denial* is the characteristic defense against shame.⁵ Denial signifies not the dishonesty of lying but rather the self-deception that Sartre termed *mauvaise foi* — "the attempt to flee what one cannot flee, to flee what one is."⁶

Individuals disabled by shame tell lies, but they are not liars. To be disabled by shame means to be unable to be honest *with oneself*. Shame blinds to shame itself — one reason why the terms and the concept, shame's naming and its experiencing, tend to fall apart, to be sundered by the very namelessness that springs from shame as an experience of nothingness. It is the abandonment of "simple truths" that entails the need for "vital lies."⁷

THE INTER-PERSONAL:
NEEDING OTHERS AND MUTUALITY

Such an indescribable experience of nothingness, so well concealed even from self, of course cuts one off from others. The characteristic judgment associated with disablement by shame runs: "No one can possibly know how I feel, for no one has ever felt this way." Uniqueness sets off. The resulting isolation is rarely splendid, but it may prove terminal. Those mired in shame suffer terminal uniqueness.

Paradoxically, however, the sense of isolated separateness can lay the foundation for the bridge across which shame may be healed. For such uniqueness becomes too painful to bear, and that very pain can open the sufferer's eyes not only to the reality of the human need for others but also to its specification in the mode of mutuality. One reason why shame is good, one reason why "shameless" is an epithet, lies in that understanding. We attain full humanity only through those realities that we get only by giving, that we bestow only by being open to receive. The experience of shame thus teaches that and how human beings need each other in order to become whole.

ENOUGH-NESS

Both shame and its healing connect with sufficiency — with the sense of *enough*. Appropriately, then, shame seems specified most sharply in all forms of addiction. Addiction signals the failure of enough-ness.

Although the refusal of "enough" hallmarks modern identity, a fascination with *boundaries* has emerged as characteristic of post-modernism. Parallel experience in the healing of shame seems to suggest that "only when however we are becomes good enough do we become free to be our very best."[8] The deeper meanings of that truth apply to more than the experience of addiction, but it seems likely that those who work in the field of addiction treatment may be the first to discover them. And they may thus discover the responsibility of making what they learn available to others, to the larger culture.

RELATIONSHIP TO "THE SPIRITUAL" AND VIRTUE — LIGHT ON CO-DEPENDENCE

For "being responsible" is not an evil concept, nor is needing others some kind of illness. Shame has to do with *being*, and therefore with those qualities the ancients termed "virtue."[9] Although this is but one source of shame's claim to a profound relationship with "the spiritual," it affords the title that merits direct attention here. The rediscovery of shame serves to offset the recent intrusion into even therapeutic understandings of the narcissistic, me-first fixations of the larger contemporary cultural context.

Those who love or live with someone afflicted by a malady such as alcoholism suffer very real pain and shame, and those who awaken sensitivity to that specific shame merit praise. But blithe inattention to the spirit of the age that has spawned the concept of "co-dependency," combined with an inadequate understanding of shame, have together issued in far too many treatments that serve mainly to render as "sick" such qualities as loyalty and commitment. If the first spiritual insight involves acceptance of one's own flawed reality, then the first spiritual response involves meeting another's defect not with the labeling blame that distances but with the compassionate pity that unites.[10]

Proper attention to shame may lead to a rediscovery of virtue. Meanwhile, as several of the articles herein attest, sensitivity to the sources of disabling shame can free, if itself freed from the blinding trammels of the narcissistic vocabulary of this passing moment. "Feeling responsible" need not signify sickness. By reminding of both-and-ness and recalling to its acceptance, shame's pointing to *enough* may help restore to sanity. And the articles that follow seem enough to begin that process.

NOTES

1. Helen Merrell Lynd, *On Shame and the Search for Identity*, London, 1958; *cf.* also Ernest Kurtz, *Shame and Guilt*, Center City, MN, 1981.

2. *Cf.* Terry Eagleton, *Literary Theory: An Introduction*, Minneapolis, 1983; Michael Goldberg, *Theology and Narrative*, Nashville, 1982; Paul Ricoeur, *Time and Narrative*, vol. 1, Chicago, 1984, vol. 2, Chicago, 1985; Robert Scholes and Robert Kellog, *The Nature of Narrative*, Oxford, 1966; Paul Veyne, *Writing History*, Middletown, CT, 1985.

3. Gerhart Piers and Milton Singer, *Shame and Guilt*, Springfield, IL., 1953; Helen Merrell Lynd, *On Shame and the Search for Identity*, London, 1958; Carl D. Schneider, *Shame, Exposure, and Privacy*, Boston, 1977; Gershen Kaufman, *Shame: The Power of Caring*, Cambridge, 1980; Ernest Kurtz, *Shame and Guilt*, Center City, MN, 1981; Janine Chasseguet-Smirgel, *The Ego Ideal*, New York, 1985; Susan Miller, *The Shame Experience*, Hillsdale, NJ, 1985.

4. *Cf.* John Mack in Margaret H. Bean, Edward J. Khantzian, John E. Mack,

George E. Vaillant, Norman E. Zinberg, *Dynamic Approaches to the Understanding and Treatment of Alcoholism*, New York, 1981; Christopher Lasch, *The Culture of Narcissism*, New York, 1978, and *The Minimal Self*, New York, 1984; on the Jungian perception *re* "spirits," *cf.* Ernest Kurtz, *Not-God: A History of Alcoholics Anonymous*, Hazelden, 1979.

5. Helen Block Lewis, *Shame and Guilt in Neurosis*, New York, 1971.

6. The classic work on shame remains Jean-Paul Sartre, *Being and Nothingness;* for useful insight, *cf.* the also-classic William Barrett, *Irrational Man*, New York, 1958.

7. *Cf.* Daniel Goleman, *Vital Lies, Simple Truths*, New York, 1985.

8. Gershen Kaufman, *Shame: The Power of Caring*, Cambridge, 1980, p. 129; on the modern/post-modern point, *cf*, Arthur C. Danto, *The Philosophical Disenfranchisement of Art*, New York, 1987.

9. *Cf.* Alasdair MacIntyre, *After Virtue*, Notre Dame, 1981; and, for a usefully critical perspective on MacIntyre, Don S. Browning, *Religious Thought and the Modern Psychologies*, Philadelphia, 1987.

10. *Cf.* James Joyce, *Portrait of the Artist as a Young Man*, p. 239; also Donald P. McNeill, Douglas A. Morrison, Henri J. M. Nouman, *Compassion*, New York, 1982; Browning, as cited; Miguel de Unamuno, *Tragic Sense of Life*, New York, 1954; and Paul V. Robb, S. J., "Conversion as a Human Experience," in *Studies in the Spirituality of Jesuits*, vol. 14, no. 3. (May 1982).

Shame and Guilt: Definitions, Processes and Treatment Issues with AODA Clients

Ronald T. Potter-Efron, PhD, MSW

SUMMARY. The primary characteristics of shame and guilt are compared and contrasted. The general treatment of each of these issues is discussed. Positive functions, defenses, origins, and the nature of the failure experience are noted.

INTRODUCTION

Shame and guilt are interactive aspects of the human condition that are deeply involved in the development and treatment of alcoholism and chemical dependency. Of the two concepts, guilt has been studied more frequently. Guilt is central to the classical Freudian model of human psychological development; in this model guilt serves to control the basic aggressive and sexual impulses of the individual. There is also a rich literary tradition dealing with the problem of guilt. Shakespeare's Lady Macbeth, Hawthorne's Reverend Dimmesdale (*The Scarlet Letter*) and Dostoyevsky's Rasknolnikov (*Crime and Punishment*) testify to the fascination and power of guilt in Western society. The concept of shame has emerged much more recently in the works of scholars and clinicians, including the pioneering efforts of Piers and Singer in 1953. Several excellent studies of shame have been written within the last decade (Kurtz, Kaufman & Schneider).

Ronald T. Potter-Efron is affiliated with the Midelfort Clinic in Eau Claire, WI.

7

Shame and guilt strongly affect alcoholics and their families. Shamed persons may attempt to hide their disgrace both from others and from themselves, contributing to the strength of denial in these families. Shame keeps the family from seeking help, erodes self-worth, and produces destructive secrets that cannot heal. Guilt may circulate freely between alcoholic and family members, so that everyone begins to feel responsible for the pain of others. Unattended, overwhelming guilt and shame tend to drive the alcoholic to drink more and the family to accept his drinking behavior.

Shame and guilt issues can be treated in the context of alcohol and chemical dependency programs. Working through these issues may help the addicted individual make a stronger commitment to sobriety, plus lessening the likelihood for relapse. Family members may also be helped to understand and manage codependent guilt and shame, freeing them from irrational feelings of overresponsibility and inadequacy.

CENTRAL CHARACTERISTICS OF SHAME AND GUILT

Shame and guilt are both commonly experienced as painful states of awareness that involve physical, mental and possibly spiritual discomfort. Frequently an individual suffers both shame and guilt simultaneously, making it difficult to distinguish between them. Nevertheless, shame and guilt are distinct and separate experiences. It is essential that the therapist be able to recognize these differences because the individual primarily encountering shame needs different treatment than someone whose central issues are based in guilt.

A comparison between the central characteristics of shame and guilt is provided in Table I.

Shame: A Failure of the Whole Self

A young woman dresses carefully for an important day-long job interview. All goes well until just after lunch when she sees herself in a mirror and realizes there is a small spot on her dress. She is suddenly swept up in a wave of despair, believing that everybody will now know that she does not deserve the new job

TABLE I: Primary Characteristics of Shame and Guilt

CENTRAL TRAIT	SHAME	GUILT
Failure	of being; falling short of goals; of whole self	of doing; of moral self
Primary Feelings	Inadequate, deficient, worthless, exposed, disgusting, disgraced	bad, wicked, evil, remorseful
Precipitating Event	unexpected, possibly trivial event	actual or contemplated violation of values
Primary Response	psychological: facial blush, eyes down, etc.	cognitive: awareness of being responsible
	affective: strong emotional response	behavioral--focus on actions
Involvement of Self	Total self image involved: "how could I have done that?"	partial--self image: "How could I have done that?
Central Fear	of abandonment, not belonging	of punishment
Origins	Positive identification with parents	need to control aggressive impulses
Primary Defenses	Desire to hide (withdrawal), denial, rage, perfectionism, grandiosity, shamelessness	Obsessive thought pattern, paranoid thinking, intellectualization, rationalization, seek excessive punishment
Positive Functions	Awareness of limits of human condition, discovery of separate self, sense of modesty, identification with community, mastery, autonomy	Sublimation, moral behavior, initiative, reparation

and in fact should never even have been allowed to apply. For the rest of the afternoon she has difficulty making eye contact, feels exposed and vulnerable, and earnestly prays for the interview to end so she can escape. Feeling totally inadequate she proceeds, no longer able to present herself with pride and unable to accept positive feedback from others. Desperately trying to make no more mistakes, she blunders over small details, each time feeling once again her complete failure as a human being. She is ashamed and turns away from herself with disgust, expecting others to do so as well (Thrane, 148).

To feel shame is to feel nakedly exposed to the world, unprotected from critical eyes. Strongly physiological, shame brings a blush to the cheeks, forces eyes downward, and propels hands to cover the face. The experience of shame may be triggered by a relatively insignificant event; once shamed, an individual tends to remember previous shameful episodes, so that even a seemingly trivial action may lead to overwhelming feelings of shame (Kaufman, 76).

Susan Miller (1985) distinguishes between shame and several related feelings. She reserves shame for a basic feeling of inferiority. In contrast, she defines "embarrassment" as the experience of feeling undone and uncomfortably visible to others, "humiliation" as feeling forced down into a debased position, and "self-consciousness" as feeling constantly aware of the self in action (Miller, pp. 31-46). These distinctions are useful in certain circumstances, but it seems likely that in many clinical situations an individual would feel all three of the above simultaneously. Consequently, I have included elements of embarrassment, humiliation, and self-consciousness in the general description of shame. However, Miller's stress on the primary of the individual's damaged sense of self is important.

Shame represents a failure of being, a falling short of the whole self, an inability to reach goals derived from positive parent images and then internalized into the self (Piers, 14). The resulting gap between self-reality and self-ideal, especially if suddenly and unexpectedly exposed to view, results in feelings of inadequacy, deficiency and disgust. Unworthy in his own eyes, the shamed individual deeply fears abandonment by those he loves and rejection from the community as a whole. He feels unlovable because of inherent irredeemable character flaws.

Origins of Shame and the Shame-Based Individual

The potential to experience shame arises within the first 18-24 months of life (Stipek, 46; Broucek, 369; Amsterdam & Levitt). It is part of the infant's beginnings of awareness that he is a separate individual. The infant who becomes self-aware also becomes self-conscious (Amsterdam & Levitt), recognizing that others can observe him. With this stage eventually comes a recognition that those who observe him may also approve or disapprove of his behavior. A shame crisis may develop when the child's "boundless exhibitionism" (Kohut, 69) meets unexpected parental disapproval, resulting in a lessening of interest, joy, and excitement in the child (Broucek, 369). Seeking approval, the child identifies with the positive goals and ideals of his nurturers. He develops a concept of his desired self (Morrison, 302) which will provide the template both for future behavior and self-worth. Having thus secured parental approval, the child can move towards becoming an autonomous human being (Erickson, 108).

A shame-based individual is someone who feels an extraordinary amount of shame deep within the "very core of self" (Kaufman, 105). These are persons who feel they are basically unacceptable to the world. They believe that they are fatally flawed, cursed, alien, monstrous, inhuman, defective. The ideal self they have developed is not a positive goal that provides opportunity to gather self-worth but a demanding tyrant forever reminding them of their failure to be "good enough." They hold themselves in contempt (Kaufman, 106).

As Kaufman notes, the origin of shame is interpersonal. He suggests that the parents of shame-based individuals display many shame generating behaviors, ranging from direct statements ("shame on you"), through overt contempt toward the child, disabling performance expectations, withdrawal of love, and emotional unavailability (Kaufman, 21-25). Ultimately the shame-based individual fears and expects abandonment and "death by emotional starvation" (Piers, 16).

It should be remembered that shame itself is not a problem. It is an excess of shame, dominating an individual, that distorts normal human development.

Defenses Against Shame

Feelings of shame may be too painful to endure, promoting the development of conscious and unconscious defenses. Probably the most widely used mechanism is *withdrawal* (Thrane, 143; Kaufman, 81-98). An individual who cannot "face up" to his shame may withdraw by averting his eyes and looking away, switching the topic of conversation, or by excusing himself from the room. Deeply shamed persons may develop a habit of emotional or physical withdrawal, becoming "runners" from life. Anonymity may also be sought by individuals who fear shame; those persons who do not stand out protect themselves from ever becoming the center of attention.

Denial is a type of withdrawal that is cited by Lewis (Lewis, 1971) as a primary defense against shame. An individual can avoid anxiety, in particular the anxiety of painful exposure of a serious failure, by turning away from the source of the problem (Lewis, 1971, p. 89). Alcoholics in denial may be shying away from looking at their shame, their failure as human beings. That is implicit in this affliction.

On occasion it becomes impossible to withdraw from shame. Perhaps without warning the individual will feel totally vulnerable or that he is about to be exposed. The result may be a sudden explosion of rage which insulates the individual from shame (Kaufman, 15). The victim in effect tells his tormentor, "I cannot survive exposure of my shame. I will attack you if you come any closer to it." It seems likely that some habitually angry and aggressive individuals are defending against a continual perception that others are attempting to shame them.

Another defense against shame is *perfectionism* (Kaufman, 181-98; Levin 360), an attempt to satisfy internalized goals that demand appeasement (Ward, 70). Perfectionism forces the individual to work harder and longer than his peers on any project; it serves only to delay inevitable feelings of inadequacy and incompetence that grow at the center of self-respect.

Grandiosity (Broucek, 374) represents a reaction formation against shame in which the individual conceals his pain by adopting opposing behaviors and thoughts. Instead of trying to become invisible, the grandiose person becomes overly visible. He may boast about his prowess, seek power, and hold others in contempt. He transfers his imperfections to the outside (Kohut, 489), hiding his real feelings of inferiority and emptiness (Morrison, 314).

Shamelessness, also called "counter-shame," is another reaction formation in which the individual acts out against his shame through exhibitionistic behavior (Morrison, 207-213). In sum, the grandiose person attempts to prevent anyone, especially himself, from observing the intrinsically damaged person that he believes himself to be, by appearing to be beyond shame. He acts "shamelessly" and in so doing demonstrates his shame.

Positive Functions of Shame

As noted above, to be "shameless" is not a healthy state of being. This means that the potential to feel shame must be important for the individual and community. Several positive values of shame have been reported.

The presence of shame, at least in relatively small doses, produces an acute *awareness of self and others* (Broucek, 371). It discloses the self to self (Schneider, 25), allowing the shamed individual sudden insight about who he is and how he appears to others. Shame appears to be an essential ingredient in the individuation process.

Schneider notes that shame promotes a generalized sense of *modesty* and privacy that greatly enhances human relationships. For example, a sense of modesty protects the sexual act from profanation and allows it to become linked to individualized love (Schneider, 18-20, 39-40). "When shame fails, disgust follows." (Schneider, 61).

Shame brings into focus the essential *limits of the human condition* (Kurtz, 10), since even brief moments of embarrassment remind us that we are only human, not gods. If not overwhelming, shame can lead toward a deep sense of personal humility. "Humility," a state of feeling no better or worse than others, is a positive alternative to either humiliation or grandiosity.

The ability to feel shame also *links the individual with his community*. (Thrane, 157). Normal shame is thought to originate in positive identifications with loving parents (Thrane, 162). The potential to feel shame joins the values and goals of the community with the individual.

Mastery and *Autonomy* are two other positive responses to the same stimuli that can produce shame. Mastery occurs when an individual responds to events and challenges, not with a sense of failure, but with realistic pride and a habit of competence. For example, an individual who has not achieved as highly as expected in school might respond to this situation by developing better study habits. Shame signals the individual to work harder or do something differently so that the individual can achieve a higher level and restore temporarily damaged pride.

Autonomy (Erickson) involves a positive sense of self-control and self-worth, as well as the notion of privacy. Autonomy seems most likely to occur when an individual is raised by parents who allow that child to "show off" on appropriate occasions so that the child learns that he is acceptable. Erickson indicates that a person tends either to become shamed or autonomous. It is important to realize that these are both responses to the child's need to be accepted as an independent but connected member of the community.

The Treatment of Shame: General Considerations

Shame issues in the AODA field and elsewhere are difficult to treat for several reasons. First, there has been little training for professionals in this area as compared with guilt so that shame themes may be overlooked. Secondly, clients tend to hide their shame even from their therapists: "Guilt feelings bring material into an interview, shame keeps them out" (Morrison, 300). Third, powerful defenses including rage surround and accompany shame, easily distracting the counselor from the primary problem. Fourth, shame experiences heal slowly because they represent significant blows to the core of an individual's self-concept. Enough time must be provided in the therapeutic context to insure that an individual with nakedly exposed shame will not be abandoned or neglected. Finally, it should be noted that shamed individuals already feel worthless and inadequate. Unfortunately in the field of alcohol and drug counseling, many therapists have been trained to confront the user without mercy.

There is a fundamental principle that underlies the treatment of shame: *Damage from shame begins to heal when that shame is exposed to others in a safe environment.* It is essential that a client's revelations of shame never be themselves shamed (Kaufman, 146). Instead, the individual must be treated with dignity since only in an atmosphere of respect can the client divorce himself from his own exacting expectations (Piers, 33). Many individuals exposing their shame in a therapeutic context still expect, at conscious or unconscious levels, to be rejected by the therapist (or by the treatment group). When the therapist continues to accept the client as a valued human being, the client can also begin to accept himself as worthwhile.

In addition to the relationship issues noted above, a therapist working with shame must help the client learn exactly how shame has affected his thoughts and behavior. For example, a particular individual may be quite distrustful of others while another may fear rejection from others because of shame (Ward, 71-73). Defensive strategies must be linked with shame so that the client can learn alternatives to these self-destructive tendencies (Kaufman, 149). Unmet needs obscured by shame also need to be validated (Kaufman, 148.)

Above all, the shamed individual yearns to believe that he is good enough to belong in the world. The primary task of the therapist is to convey this message to the recovering client.

Guilt: A Failure of Doing

A man who has been cited for drunken driving and causing a fatal accident reluctantly appears before the judge. He argues that he is not guilty of the latter because he was drunk at the time and did not know what he was doing. After being warned by his lawyer that his sentence will probably be lighter if he admits his guilt and shows remorse (Felson & Ribner; O'Malley & Greenberg), he pretends to do so. Two months later, while completing treatment for chemical dependency, he recognizes that he was indeed responsible for his behavior. He is strongly motivated to make amends to the family of the victim. Although not eager to be imprisoned, he accepts punishment and rededicates himself to a life of sobriety and social responsibility.

Guilt occurs when an individual touches or transgresses a boundary (Piers, 11), either anticipating or actually violating internalized societal rules or norms (Forrest, 207). Instead of falling short, as with the experience of shame, the guilty individual has gone too far. His "selfish" desires begin to threaten the web of common human relationships. Like a single fish that has strayed too far from the school, the deviating individual is drawn back towards the center. Guilt is the internal mechanism that reminds the individual that he must obey societal norms or eventually he will be punished. If those rules have already been violated, guilt drives the perpetrator to renounce his unacceptable behavior and even to attempt to repair the damage he has done.

Guilt is more cognitive and behavioral and less affective than shame. A guilty person may think obsessively about his behavior but he is less likely to blush or have other strong physical reactions. However, guilty persons may report particular physical/affective reactions such as emptiness or fear. Because guilt and innocence normally refer to specific behaviors, to be guilty of something does not usually involve a person's entire self. This may be why guilt frequently motivates an individual to take action by moving toward others while shame compels the victim to retreat. Guilt is also more quantified than shame: a relevant question is not only whether or not the individual is guilty, but how much.

Types of Guilt

Guilt appears in many forms and has many names. Because it is specific to a particular situation, it is possible to refer to sex guilt (Evans), survivor guilt (Miles & Demi), and even recovery guilt, which is guilt felt when an individual begins to recover from a significant problem, perhaps leaving others behind (Miles & Demi). A crucial distinction exists between rational and irrational guilt (Forrest, 222; Ellis). *Rational guilt* feelings emerge as an individual acts inappropriately in the current situation. This is a realistic response to harm done in the present (Hoffman: 1982, 281). Rational guilt only diminishes when the individual ceases guilt-producing behavior. Rational guilt always implies that the individual has the ability to make choices about his actions (Kurtz, 23.) *Irrational guilt*, sometimes referred to as neurotic guilt (Miles & Demi; Ellis; Stein, 26; Figarette), is a term that refers to any magnification or distortion of behavior, leading toward excessive or unnecessary guilt. Irrational guilt occurs when an individual decides that because a particular behavior he committed is bad, he is a totally bad person (Grieger & Boyd, 44). This may in turn lead to a need for excessive punishment from others as well as to unconscious self-condemnation (Stein, 26). Royce (Royce, 299), speaking directly about the guilt of the alcoholic, notes that guilt is irrational when a behavior is not really wrong, could not have been avoided, or had long since been forgiven. During therapy, many irrational guilt feelings can be traced to their childhood origins (Forrest, 222).

Guilt may develop as the result of both commissions and omissions (Hoffman: 1982, 299). Perhaps it is the latter, a failure to do something good when the opportunity arises, that leads to existential guilt, a vague term that appears to refer to an individual's failure to live up to his full human potential (Miles & Demi). Existential guilt may have no specific cause. It can lead to acute suffering and is seen essentially as a spiritual discomfort associated with one's current state of being (Carroll, 10; Buber, 60; Sternig). Existential guilt is much more difficult to relieve than rational guilt since no specific normative violation has been actually committed and yet the individual feels deeply incapable (Carroll, 158).

Origins of Guilt

Psychoanalytic therapists, beginning with Freud, believe that guilt originates in childhood as a response to the emergence of aggressive and sexual impulses (Freud; Klein). These impulses produce conflict for the child since they bring him into a potential struggle for power with his parents — a one-sided struggle he cannot win. The child is in danger of punishment or losing love (Morris). This struggle is partially resolved when the child identifies with his parents. He then develops internal prohibitions against those impulses (Freud's "super-ego"). Guilt is experienced whenever these forbidden impulses threaten to break through conscious and unconscious barriers into action (Hoffman, 1982 [June], 89). Guilt is "the condemnation of the ego by its own critical agency" (Freud, 41). Normally this guilt is useful and appears irregularly. If this critical force becomes too strong, the individual may feel chronic, unrelenting guilt (Freud, 43) that is destructive.

A second perspective is that guilt occurs primarily when an individual has indeed harmed others by his behavior (Hoffman,

1982, 281). Human beings are assumed to be positively socially oriented in this model. Bringing harm to others arouses painful stress that is experienced as guilt. Although this explanation says little about the origin of irrational guilt, it does focus interest upon current behavior and directs attention toward the positive aspects of guilt.

Positive Functions of Guilt

As with shame, a normal amount of guilt has value both for the individual and society. Freudians believe that potentially destructive sexual and aggressive energy can be redirected into socially acceptable action. This process is called *sublimation*. Feelings of guilt are considered a fundamental incentive toward creativeness and work in general (Klein, 336).

A second positive function of guilt is called *reparation* (Klein, 309), defined as a need to repair any damage done to others by the individual. The discomfort of guilt often leads first to a need to confess the behavior, secondly to accept personal responsibility for any damage to others, third to attempt to undo the damage and/or a willingness to accept punishment for the behavior, and finally to seek forgiveness from others (Thrane, 148). Completing this process allows the individual to return to good social standing in the community. In this way guilt transforms originally antisocial behavior into a celebration of community. This reparative process is particularly evident with recovering alcoholics who seek the AA community in which to begin the task of regaining social respectability.

Third, guilt feelings may lead to *altruism* and *moral behavior*, genuine sympathy toward others based on empathetic distress (Klein, 309; Hoffman, 1982; 297). In these situations, personal guilt feelings are extended through imagination. Instead of simply wishing to undo personal damage, an individual comes to want to alleviate the suffering of others regardless of its origin. The individual develops a consistent moral philosophy that both precludes harmful acts and prescribes socially binding behavior toward others.

Finally, Erickson refers to *initiative* as the positive resolution for potentially guilt inducing situations. A person with a sense of initiative has internalized moral values and emerges with the ability to engage the world constructively. He can express feelings of love and warmth without fear of punishment (Scroggs, pg. 59-60). This individual has developed a realistic sense of ambition and purpose and is prepared to assume adult roles effectively and energetically.

Defenses Against Guilt

Despite its positive functions, the feeling of guilt is uncomfortable and anxiety producing. Certain defenses have been identified that reduce this discomfort. One of these is an *obsessive thought pattern* (Lewis, 199). This is similar to the perfectionism associated with shame. By constantly thinking about things, trying to collect more and more information before acting, the obsessive thinker protects himself against taking the wrong action and then feeling guilty. An individual may also begin thinking obsessively after committing an unacceptable behavior. In these situations the repetitive thoughts partly alleviate anxiety, especially when they are linked with compulsive behavior.

Paranoid thought processes have also been linked with guilt (Lewis, 1971, pg. 91). Here the individual projects his aggressive impulses outward, giving them to others. He then may become convinced that these others want to act aggressively toward himself. Persons who have been raised in situations where any aggressive behavior is severely punished may be more vulnerable to defending against guilt through paranoid ideation.

Guilt may also be defended against by *intellectualization*, a process in which the individual cuts off most feelings (Lewis, 1971). These persons may talk a great deal about their behavior and may even be aware of guilt and yet they cannot connect these thoughts with relevant feelings or behaviors. The intellectualizer protects himself by minimizing any painful feelings that might be associated with guilt. In effect, the intellectualizer lives from his neck up; he needs to be grounded in feelings before effective change can take place.

An effective but socially damaging defense against guilt is the process of *rationalization* (Lewis, 1971), which may also be called neutralization (Mitchell & Dodder). This process occurs when an individual justifies his misbehavior by denying or minimizing its effects. For example, a batterer may deny that he injured the victim. Alternatively he may admit that he caused the injury but claim that his behavior was justified because of the previous actions of the victim. In effect, the rationalizer either denies or projects his guilt onto others, blaming them for his own behavior.

Guilt laden individuals also may defend themselves through *seeking excessive punishment*, broadly defined as actions that encourage others to punish or humiliate them. Piers uses the term "masochism" (Piers, 20) to describe this behavior, but masochism is probably too sexually oriented a concept to describe this pattern adequately. It is more correct to state that persons who feel guilty can lessen their anxiety and fear of punishment by seeking out such punishment. When this becomes habitual, an individual comes to expect punishment and to assume that he must be guilty of something at all times. The punishment seeking individual appears to get trapped in a cycle in which he must continually seek out current punishment in an effort to avoid anxiety about future punishment. As Piers notes, this individual deals with excessive guilt by enduring humiliating shame (Piers, 20).

Treatment of Guilt: General Considerations

Guilt, like shame, is a treatable condition that can be recognized and approached during AODA treatment. Counselors working with guilt must approach the individual with a nonjudgmental attitude, although acceptance of the individual does not indicate approval of his behavior (Stein, 162). One important objective is to help the individual separate his unacceptable behavior from his core identity. He needs to learn that he is responsible for but not wholly defined by his transgressions (Murphy).

Guilt alone is not an effective behavioral control (Murphy). Therefore the alcoholic who claims he will stay sober because of his guilt should be confronted with the likelihood that his guilt will only lead to more drinking if left unattended.

A general principle in the treatment of guilt is that *rational guilt is best resolved by living responsibly in the present*. For the alcoholic this means that "pathological guilt can only be resolved through sobriety and work" (Forrest, 213). The guilty alcoholic must be steered toward sobriety and a sober lifestyle in order to alleviate the rational guilt associated with alcoholic behavior.

After an individual begins living a sober lifestyle, he may then meaningfully explore his past guilt. The acts of surrender (Curlee-Salisbury, 268), confession (Thrane, 148), and making amends (Curlee-Salisbury, 269), are all associated with undoing the past guilt of the recovering alcoholic. The goal of these behaviors is forgiveness by the community, God, and self. Confession rituals may have to be repeated frequently by the recovering alcoholic as a central aspect of recovery (Forrest, 220). At the same time, it is important to help individuals recognize when they indeed have been forgiven by others or when they could not be held responsible for something that happened (Royce, 299). In this manner, the therapist, staying in reality, can direct the confessional process toward the event resolution of rational guilt.

Irrational guilt will normally be the last type to address during the recovery process since it is often deeply embedded in messages received in childhood. The therapeutic approach here is to trace back these messages to their source, expose their unreasonable characteristics, and help the client construct new, more flexible and reasonable messages that can guide him as an adult. This process is time consuming but worthwhile when an individual can be freed from nagging irrational guilt. It is also important to remember that irrational guilt blends imperceptibly into shame and the basic sense of self may need to be examined.

CONCLUSION

Shame and guilt feelings both contribute to the pain of the alcoholic and the alcoholic family. These feelings precede the disease, often developing in early childhood, eroding the individual's sense of worth, making him vulnerable to the flight from reality that is alcoholism. Then, once alcoholism takes over, the victim may feel even more shame and guilt because of his continuing shortcomings. Without effective intervention, shame and guilt feelings drive the individual toward more drinking in an effort to relieve that pain. Fortunately, sobriety can break this self-perpetuating pattern.

Shame has been defined here as a failure of being, a painful emotional sense of falling short that attacks the core of self-concept. Attempts to defend against an overwhelming shame include withdrawal, grandiosity, perfectionism, and rage. The capacity to feel a moderate amount of shame does have positive value for the individual, reminding him of his goals in life, and the limits of the human condition, connecting him with others, and providing a barrier between public and private life that gives greater meaning to the latter. The general goal of therapy with shame is to provide an atmosphere where shame related concerns may be exposed in a safe environment. As shame becomes manageable an individual regains a sense of belonging in the world. He gives up old feelings of being alien and learns that he is acceptable as an individual. By dealing with shame the recovering alcoholic, with the help of the AA community, eventually transforms feelings of humiliation to true humility and rejoins the human race.

Guilt has been defined here as a failure of doing, a transgression of the values or norms of society. Guilt feelings tell the individual that he has done or is thinking of doing something wrong, immoral, or unethical. Moderate guilt feelings enhance pro-social behavior, lead toward the development of empathy and altruism and direct the guilty person toward actions that undo any damage to others he has caused. Two primary types of guilt have been identified: rational and irrational. Rational guilt occurs in proportion to actual harm done by others. Rational guilt is assuaged by confession, reparation of damages, and by living a lifestyle consistent with one's values. Irrational guilt usually is the result of early parental messages and occurs whenever an individual feels guilty about behavior over which he had no control or which was not actually harmful to others, or when the individual wrongfully believes he is a totally bad person because he has done something wrong. Treatment for irrational guilt usually requires relatively long-term therapy. Defenses against overwhelming guilt include neutralization, obsessional thinking and seeking excessive punishment.

Shame and guilt issues offer alcohol counselors an opportunity to help their clients make meaningful long-term commitments to sobriety and sober living, and to address the causes and consequences of drinking.

REFERENCES

Amsterdam, Beulah & Levitt, Morton, "Consciousness of Self and Painful Self-Consciousness," *Psychoanalytic Study of the Child*, 35, 67-83, 1980.

Bard, James, *Rational Emotive Therapy in Practice*, Chicago: Research Press, 1980.

Blum, Eva & Blum, Richard, *Alcoholism*, York, PA: Jossey-Bass, 1967.

Broucek, Francis, "Shame and Its Relationship to Early Narcissistic Developments." *International Journal of Psycho-Analysis*, 63 (3), 369-378, 1982.

Buber, Martin, "Guilt and Guilt Feelings," in Morris, Herbert (ed.), *Guilt and Shame*, Belmont, CA: Wadsworth, 58-81, 1971.

Carroll, John, *Guilt*, London; Routledge and Kegan Paul.

Curlee-Salisbury, Joan, "Perspectives on Alcoholics Anonymous," In Estes, Nada & Heinmann, M. Edith, *Alcoholism*, St. Louis: Mosby, 266-273, 1977.

Ellis, Albert, *Reason and Emotion in Psychotherapy*, Secaucus, NJ: Lyle Stuart, 1975.

Erickson, Erik, *Identity: Youth and Crisis*, NY, Norton Press, 1968.

Evans, Ronald, "Hostility and Sex Guilt: Perceptions of Self and Others as a Function of Gender and Sex Role Orientation," *Sex Roles*, 10 (3-4), 207-215, 1984 (ret).

Felson, Richard & Ribner, Stephen, "An Attributional Approach to Accounts and Sanctions for Criminal Violence," *Social Psychology Quarterly*, 44 (2), 137-142, 1981 (June).

Fingarette, Herbert, "Real Guilt and Neurotic Guilt," in Morris, Herbert (ed.), *Guilt and Shame*, Belmont, CA: Landsworth Pub. 82-94, 1971.

Fisher, Sebern, "Identity of Two: The Phenomenology of Shame in Borderline Development and Treatment," *Psychotherapy*, 22 (1), 101-109, 1985 (Sp).

Forrest, Gary, *Alcoholism, Narcissism and Psychopathology*, Springfield: Ch. Thomas, 1983.

Freud, Sigmund, *The Ego and the Id*, NY: Norton, 1960

Freud, Sigmund, "Origin of the Sense of Guilt," in Morris, Herbert (ed.), *Guilt and Shame*, Belmont, CA: Wadsworth Pub., 54-58, 1971.

Gomberg, Edith & Lisansky, Judith, "Antecedents of Alcohol Problems in Women," in Wilsnack, Sharon & Beckman, Linda (eds.), *Alcohol Problems in Women*, NY: Guilford, 1984.

Grieger, Russell & Boyd, John, *Rational Emotive Therapy*, NY: Nostrand and Reinhold, 1980.

Hoffman, Martin, "Affect and Moral Development," in Cicchetti, Dante & Hesse, Petra, *Emotional Development*, 16, 1982 (June).

Hoffman, Martin, "Development of Pro-Social Motivation; Empathy and Guilt," in Eisenberg, Nancy (ed.), *The Development of Pro-Social Behavior*, NY: Academic Press, 281-314, 1982.

Jackson, J. G., "Alcoholism Fathers As Compared With Adult Daughters of Non-Alcoholic Fathers," *Dissertation Abstracts International*, 46 (1), 338-B, 1985.

Kaufman, Gershen, *Shame: The Power of Caring*, Cambridge, MA: Schenkman, 1980.

Klein, Melanie, *Love, Guilt and Reparation*, NY: Delacorte Pr, 1975.

Kohut, Heinz, *The Search for Self*, Ornstein, Paul (ed.), NY: International U. Press, 1978.

Kruger, D. W., "Neurotic Behavior and the Alcoholic," in E. Pattison & E. Kaufman (eds.), *Encyclopedic Handbook of Alcoholism*, NY: Gardner Press, 1982, 598-606.

Kurtz, Ernest, *Shame and Guilt: Characteristics of the Dependency Cycle*, Center City, MN: Hazelden Press, 1981.

Levin, Sidney "The Psychoanalysis of Shame," *International Journal of Psychoanalysis*, 52, 355-361, 1971.

Lewis, Helen, "Sex Differences in Superego Mode as Related to Sex Differences in Psychiatric Illness," *Social Science and Medicine*, 12B, 199-205, 1978 (July).

Lewis, Helen, *Shame and Guilt in Neurosis*, New York: International Universities Press, 1971.

Lynd, Helen Merrill, *On Shame and the Search for Identity*, New York: Science Editions, 1961.

Miles, Margaret & Demi, Alice, "Toward the Development of a Theory of Bereavement Guilt: Sources of Guilt in Bereaved Parents," *Journal of Death and Dying*, 14, (4), 299-314, 1983-1984.

Miller, Susan, *The Shame Experience*, Hillsdale, N.J.: L. Erlbaum Associates, 1985.

Mitchell, Jim & Dodder, Richard, "Types of Neutralization and Types of Delinquency," *Journal of Youth and Adolescence*, 12 (4), 307-318, 1983 (Aug).

Mollon, Phil, "Shame in Relation to Narcissistic Disturbance," *British Journal of Medical Psychology*, 57, 207-214, 1984.

Morrison, Andrew, "Shame, Ideal Self and Narcissism," *Contemporary Psychoanalysis* 19, (2), 295-318, 1983 (April).

Morrison, Andrew, "Working With Shame in Psychoanalytic Treatment," *Journal of American Psychoanalytic Association*, 32 (3), 479-505, 1984.

Murphy, Kevin, "A Cognitive-Behavior Approach to Client Anxiety, Anger, Depression, and Guilt," *Personnel and Guidance Journal*, 59 (4), 202-205, 1980 (Dec).

O'Malley, Michael & Greenberg, Jerald, "Sex Differences in Restoring Justice: The Down Payment Effect," *Journal of Research in Personality*, 7 (2), 174-185, 1983 (June).

Piers, Gerhart & Singer, Milton, *Shame and Guilt*, Springfield, Ill: Ch. Thomas, 1953.

Prosen, Mel; Clark, David C.; Harrow, Martin & Fawcett, Jan, "Guilt and Conscience in Major Depressive Disorders," *American Journal of Psychiatry*, 140 (7), 839-844, 1983 (June).

Royce, James, *Alcohol Problems and Alcoholism*, NY: Free Press, 1981.

Schneider, Carl, *Shame, Exposure and Privacy*, Boston: Beacon Press, 1977.

Scroggs, James R., *Letting Love In*, Englewood Cliffs, NJ: 1978.

Stein, Edward, *Guilt: Theory and Therapy*, Philadelphia: Westminster Press, 1968.

Sternig, Philip, "Finding Meaning Through Existential Guilt," *International Forum for Logotherapy*, 7 (11), 46-49, 1984 (Spl. Sum).

Stipek, Dorothy, "A Developmental Analysis of Pride and Shame," *Human Development*, 1983, 26, 42-54.

Thrane, Gary, "Shame," *Journal of the Theory of Social Behavior*, 9 (2), 139-166, 1979 (July).

Ward, Henry, "Aspects of Shame in Analysis," *American Journal of Psychoanalysis*, 32, 62-73, 1972.

The Process of Healing Shame

Bruce Fischer, MA

SUMMARY. This paper discusses the process of healing internalized shame and considers some of the practical aspects of clinical work with shame based clients. Special attention is given to discussing alcoholic and adult children of alcoholics. This paper will focus on working with a client via individual therapy; however, the stages presented can be applied to a client in group and family therapy or an individual's growth within a self-help group.

> It takes two to speak the truth,
> one to speak, and another to hear.
>
> *Henry David Thoreau*

> In the Midst of Winter
> I Finally Learned there was in Me
> an Invincible Summer
>
> *Albert Camus*

THE CONTEXT OF HEALING

The quotes listed above synthesize the ideas developed in this paper. Each of us has the resources inside to adequately cope with our shame, yet we need another to listen as we discover the truth about ourselves. All change occurs in context; shame needs a context of disciplined support in which to change. The context must be warm but not patronizing, firm but not harsh, and emo-

---

Bruce Fischer is a licensed psychologist in private practice in Minneapolis and on the faculty at the Alcohol and Drug Counselor Education Program at the Department of Family Social Science at the University of Minnesota.

tional but not maudlin or hysterical. In addition to considering the process of change attention will be given to illustrating the context of change.

It is the author's contention that a fairly predictable process is evident in the successful healing of shame. This section will describe this process and how therapists can respectfully follow and guide a client through this process.

The stages of the process are listed in the following chart.

The Stages of the Healing Process of Internalized Shame

1. Develop a trusting relationship with the client.
2. Identify and support the defenses used to protect clients from their shame.
3. Identify and label the shame in the present.
4. Connect the shame to the past, particularly the family and its rules and the roles learned during childhood.
5. Support the client in emotionally experiencing the pain and related shame in the present.
6. Identify the specific losses and support the client in grieving.
7. Identify past and present resources.
8. Help clients decide how to utilize the resources available to them.
9. Assist the client in crystallizing a new identity formed around esteem, capability and feeling lovable and worthy.

While these stages are somewhat predictable, the author wishes to emphasize that human beings tend to function in a somewhat nonlinear fashion, particularly when fear and shame are involved; hence, the idea of "two steps forward and one backwards" may be a useful and comforting thought for the therapist as well as for the client. Frequently the therapist's shame becomes involved in the treatment process if the client's progress does not match the therapist's expectations. This may deteriorate into a situation where the therapist becomes disappointed or angry with the client as a defense against the therapist's own shame. The client ultimately should be the one to determine the pace at which they move through this process. It is important to note that people do not necessarily move through the entire process in one therapeutic experience. Clients leave therapy and may return to the same or another therapist in weeks, months or even years.

These stages are discussed in this paper in terms of individual therapy; they may be experienced between a client and a therapy group, a self-help group, or within any healthy relationship. Frequently, however, clients with severe internalized shame will need some professional assistance beyond self-help groups and supportive friends and family.

THE PROCESS OF HEALING SHAME

Listed below are the stages of healing shame. Each stage will be discussed and important clinical considerations will be noted.

Develop a Trusting Relationship with the Client

While this sounds simple, it is, in fact, a process which takes time, some skill, and much patients on the part of the therapist. Shame-based clients are not particularly trusting; however, some may appear trusting in an effort to be "good clients," and to win the therapist's approval. It is important for helpers to remember that the client will at best be ambivalent about getting close and trusting.

It may be useful to talk openly with clients about their fears. Some of the fears clients frequently report are: fear of being judged or rejected, fear of becoming dependent on the therapist, fear of "going crazy," fear of crying, and fear of going "out of control." Generally at this point in the process it is best not to provide reassurance to the client. Premature reassurance with shame-based clients usually decreases the client's trust in the therapist. For example, what the client might think and not say is, "If you really knew me, you wouldn't say that." What may be more fruitful than reassurance is to explore more fully the client's fears. The author often uses the question, "What would happen then?" to further the client's exploration.

Rather than talking about whether or not a client trusts, it is generally more helpful to talk about the degree of trust a client has. Bear in mind that trust, particularly early in therapy, is highly variable and may easily be damaged.

The therapist should be careful not to unintentionally agree with and support a client's shame and self-criticism. For example, a client might say, "You probably think I'm crazy; I don't know what has come over me. I just don't know what to do with my marriage." In this situation, the therapist must be careful not to provide premature reassurance while at the same time not agree with the client's statement that he is "crazy."

Skilled therapists can easily recognize a client's shame, even in the initial visit. This is usually based on nonverbal cues such as avoidance of eye contact, hanging the head, or the obvious defenses employed against shame, as well as direct statements made by the client. At this point it is generally not helpful to directly identify and label the client's shame until a relationship has had time to develop. Moving too quickly to discuss the shame increases the client's experience of defectiveness, powerlessness, and transparency; in other words, the client's experience of shame. The client's internal experience is likely to be, "Oh, no. He can already see that there is something wrong with me, it's so obvious."

It is critical that the therapist not personalize the fact that the client does not easily trust. After all, difficulty with establishing and maintaining a trusting and intimate relationship is part of the reason the client is in therapy. The therapist must learn to accept the client's mistrust and suspicion as one of the client's best defenses.

Identify and Support the Defenses Used to Protect Clients from Their Shame

This step involves assisting clients to understand and value the ways in which they have survived emotionally. Defenses against the experience of shame have been identified by Kaufman (1985). Some of these defenses are arrogance, blaming, withdrawing or disconnecting, controlling, and perfectionism; these may be redefined as behaviors which have been adaptive. That is, these behaviors have helped in coping with severe internalized shame. Paradoxically, it may be fruitful for the therapist to encourage the client to continue to use these defenses "whenever necessary" for survival. The author often makes use of the Ericksonian techniques of utilizing, redefining, and prescribing as a part of the therapeutic process. For example, a client may be encouraged to, "continue to be distant, cautious and possibly even critical and mistrustful until you are ready to talk about what you are thinking. After all, we have only recently met and you have absolutely no reason to trust me. So check me out to make sure you are safe with me."

Frequently these "therapeutic prescriptions" serve to increase a client's sense of security with the therapist and at the same time increase the client's sense of internal power and valuing of self and his natural abilities. Examination of the defenses and how they were learned in the family of origin begins to reduce defensiveness. It is important to let the client know that as the therapist you do not intend to take away the client's defenses. Rather, you hope to provide alternatives which they may find more useful in their present life. Given an internal awareness of alternatives, clients will begin to experience a sense of power within themselves. This is one way of reducing internalized shame.

Identifying and Labeling the Shame in the Present

Once the client has some trust and has experienced the therapist's support for their defenses, the therapist may begin to directly identify and label the client's shame. This must be done in a respectful but matter-of-fact fashion. Care must be taken not to pity the client. The therapist's use of language is critical. The client's emotion must be accurately reflected by the therapist. It is important not to minimize or amplify the client's feelings. This requires the therapist to have a wide vocabulary which will communicate a variety of different levels of emotional intensity of shame. Some of the words the author uses to label various levels of shame are modest, anxious, embarrassed, self-conscious, ashamed, and humiliated.

In addition to identifying the client's shame, other emotions may be notable and need to be identified and verbalized, particularly the emotions of anger and fear. The skill of accurately identifying their own emotion may be limited in many shame-based clients. This emotional blunting may be understood as a defense. After all, if you stop feeling, you stop feeling shame. Unfortunately, feeling joy and happiness and other "positive" emotions remain unexperienced as well. Therefore, out of necessity, therapists working with shame-based clients often spend a great deal of time teaching clients how to identify, label and verbalize what they are feeling. Kaufman (1985) identified that clients often experience affect-shame binds. Basically, the client feels ashamed because of experiencing a particular emotion; such as anger. Some clients feel ashamed of experiencing any emotion. The client's internal response to this bind is generally to "shut down" and engage defensive behavior to protect the self from further torment. Hence, they may blame others, strive to compensate by working harder, or try to become a better person. In any case, the emotions are not directly experienced and expressed with another person.

In this stage of therapy the therapist must be observant of the client's behavior and comment directly on the client's shame when it is being experienced. This may be done directly by interpreting the clients behavior, or simply asking the client what he is feeling. When directly labeling the client's shame, it is critical to identify how you have reached your interpretation. For example, "I see you looking down and your voice has dropped so that it's difficult to hear you. I wonder if you are feeling ashamed." Describing the behavior you are using to reach your conclusion helps the client feel less "transparent" and also gives the client a clearer understanding of how others see them.

Once the client begins to experience and label the shame in the present, it is critical to assist the client in staying actively involved in the therapeutic relationship. The client will automatically employ the unconscious defenses which he has used to cope with shame in the past. Commonly used defenses are: changing the subject, minimizing feelings, withdrawal, self-blame, and dissociation. The task of the therapist here is to gently coax the client, as he experiences the shame, into maintaining a connection with the therapist. The client will experience considerable ambivalence about this. At this point the therapist must, in a supportive way, challenge the client to stick with the experience of shame and to talk about it with the therapist. This is the most important skill to be taught to the client in the entire course of therapy: the skill of staying with the shame, without becoming paralyzed, and talking to another human being.

Connect the Shame to the Past, Particularly the Family and Its Rules and the Roles Learned During Childhood

Typically the client is unconsciously living out unhealthy family rules learned during childhood; these rules should be identified and discussed. Time must be given to assist the client in understanding some of the origins of shame. Understanding the origins of the shame reduces self-blame. Increasing awareness can be accomplished by the client recalling and discussing experiences from childhood, journaling, visiting the family to observe the family communication, and using educational resources. The author has found educational audio-tapes (Fischer, 1986) particularly effective in increasing client awareness of the dynamics of shame and the process of healing. All of these help the client to understand who they are and how they came to be that person.

In the case of recovering alcoholics, often at this point they realize how they may have learned in their families to use chemicals to cope with emotional pain. One caution to bear in mind in this phase of therapy is that frequently clients try to go back to the family and change them or to educate the family as to what they are learning about themselves. While this may be useful later, the author has found it effective to "restrain" the client at this point. The client's helpfulness can be seen as both codependency and/or a way to bargain with the losses of childhood by attempting to replace what was lost. Attempts to educate and change the family are common and may be obvious or indirect and subtle. Obvious attempts are telling the family how they felt as a child, giving them helpful feedback, and simply telling family members how they should behave. Indirect attempts include sending the family books and reading materials, talking about how siblings felt as they grew up, and talking about current sibling problems.

Support the Client in Emotionally Experiencing the Pain and Related Shame in the Present

From discussing the family of origin the client often begins to experience deep feelings. The client needs to be encouraged to stay with the emotion. At this point in therapy the author often asks the question, "Do you remember feeling this way as a child?" Usually the client recalls a similar feeling and with a little prompting is able to emotionally relive an experience. In most cases the client willingly shares the recalled experience and with a little encouragement is able to allow himself to feel for the child within him. After the client has learned to stay with himself emotionally, the emotion needs to be validated, empathized with, given meaning and put in context. At this point it is important for the therapist to validate the emotional experience of the client. Likewise, self-help groups, particularly Adult Children of Alcoholics are useful in this regard. Clients frequently at this point tend to minimize their own needs and feelings. Statements like, "I was too sensitive" or "I was just selfish" are commonly made by clients in an effort to protect themselves from the painful truth, the fact that many of their basic emotional needs were not met as children. The client will likely have very intense emotion with this realization. These emotions, including rage, hatred, fear, shame, pain and loss, need to be experienced and expressed.

This pain of the child within is the basis of one's shame. Until this connection to the pain of the child within is made, the shame and the resultant defenses will remain intact. In short, the present experience of shame in the therapeutic relationship must be emotionally connected to events of the past.

Identify the Losses and Support the Client in Grieving

Once the client begins to suffer the emotion of the past they will recognize having been emotionally isolated from others. There will also be recognition of the extent of their own dissociation, in other words the extent to which they have lost themselves. These losses, the unmet needs, need to be validated and supported first by the therapist to enable the client to do it for himself. There is, at this point, a profound paradox. In the middle of suffering through one's isolation, there is the discovery of the fact that this experience is being shared by another human being. Furthermore, they are sharing the experience with themselves.

It is critical that the therapist allow himself to be emotionally connected in the therapeutic relationship at this point. That the therapist may feel sad at this time is natural; this may be shared with the client in a way that emotionally bonds with the client, without shifting the client's attention to the therapist's emotional state. An example of such a response would be, "As I listen to how alone you felt as a child I feel sad that you were not able to share those feelings with anyone." It is in this moment that healing occurs.

At this point, it is beneficial for the client to realize the therapist feels and is not ashamed of it. The therapist's emotional response must be verbalized and genuine. The therapist's inability to be genuine will limit the therapeutic outcome; hence, incomplete grieving over losses in the therapist's life will interfere with the therapeutic process. This underscores the need for therapists to have done their own "work" before working with shame-based clients.

Identify Resources, Both Past and Present

This phase "spontaneously" grows out of grieving. In addition to discovering the compassion of the therapist the client often begins to realize that others are available. In fact, others may have been available in the past, but the client was not able to accept this because of the shame of wanting and needing support. Clients will begin to have memories of times that they were cared for. These memories should be defined as valuable gifts within themselves which they may access and experience whenever they feel the need. For example, a client was crying about how her mother was critical and failed to provide her with emotional support or nurturance. As she cried, she asked to sit on the floor in front of a portable kerosene heater which was lit and near the chair she was in. She sat in front of the heater, her eyes glazed for a while (dissociation) and she began to recall a number of times with her grandmother at a cabin. She remembered sitting in front of the fire with her grandmother brushing her hair and talking with her. She again began to cry, but this time the tears were "bittersweet;" she said she had not remembered those times for twenty years.

Help Clients Decide How to Utilize the Resources Available to Them

It seems logical that as clients discover that people care about them, they would rush out and begin to share themselves with those who care. Unfortunately, this is not always the case; it may be necessary for the therapist to assist the client in developing a systematic plan to use the resources available. Unless clients generalize the skills learned in the therapeutic relationship, they will remain dependent upon the therapist. The therapist must gently encourage risk taking with others. This includes talking with spouse, friends, the family of origin, and members of support or self-help groups. In most cases, the client has some network of support which has been severely underused.

If a support network does not exist or is severely limited the therapist may assist the client in developing one. Self-help groups are exceptionally helpful here. Clients should be encouraged to "shop around" for a group in which they feel "comfortable" or, at best, a group in which they feel "least uncomfortable." Shame-based clients initially avoid group contact, and commonly they "forget" to get a sponsor. Having a sponsor is critical to effective utilization of the self-help program. Often the sponsor is the link to assist the client in having a sense of "belonging" in the group. Therapists should not be threatened by the sponsor. The sponsor is generally one of the therapist's best allies and should be viewed as such.

The task of the therapist in this phase is to reduce the client's dependence on the therapist and to initiate the process of leave taking. While it may take some time it is best to begin talking about it with the client.

Assist the Client in Crystallizing a New Identity Formed Around Esteem, Capability, and Feeling Lovable and Worthy

As clients begin to experience the resources within themselves they will begin to have a different sense of themselves. This "new" self must be verbalized. It is important for the clients to hear themselves say these things. Assignments such as requiring clients to describe their strengths and weaknesses, or asking others for feedback on their strengths often help the client to crystallize a more positive sense of self. Self-help groups or therapy groups can be beneficial by providing clients with positive feedback on which to build a new sense of self.

These affirmations of the "new" are critical and must be encouraged and supported by the therapist. Clients may experience some shame in response to making self-affirmations. This should be talked about and, in some cases, the therapist may find it beneficial to share how he feels in response to hearing the client's affirmations. For example, a therapist might say, "I feel delighted you are able to say that you are proud of how you handled yourself during your visit to your parents. I am proud of you!" This personal validation of the client is absolutely critical to the therapeutic process. The therapist must be able to, in a genuine, intimate, and supportive manner, praise the client. Traditional analytic therapists tend to remain too detached from the client at this point in the process. To be effective, the therapist must again risk intimacy with the client. This phase of therapy, while highly rewarding, is difficult because the therapy is winding down and both therapist and client will recognize that termination is forthcoming. The process of termination is likely to be somewhat painful for the client, and possibly the therapist, and these feelings should be explored and verbalized with the client.

GUIDELINES FOR WORKING
WITH SHAME-BASED CLIENTS

Listed below are several practical suggestions which the author has found helpful to bear in mind when working with shame-based clients. While these "rules of thumb" are useful for most cases there will, however, be exceptions. Because of the intimate nature of therapy with shame-based clients each therapist must ultimately acquire his own set of rules and guidelines which work for him in relation to these clients.

1. Avoid pity for the client at all cost. It is patronizing and it infers that clients are helpless in relation to their shame. There is a time for support and a time for compassion, but support and

compassion are very different from pity. There is also a time to be firm with clients. Asking "What do you want?" and "What are you going to do about it?" are helpful responses when a client is convinced they are powerless. In some cases, to not ask those questions is to neglect and pity people; to allow them to remain not responsible for themselves. Many clients need to be challenged to learn self-discipline, particularly in the area of self-care. Self-help groups may inadvertently teach people to use self-pity as a defense. This happens when clients learn to say they are powerless and not make a distinction between an addiction and their shame. It is the author's contention that we need not be powerless in relation to our shame. We can learn to talk openly about it, endure it without being ashamed, ask for what we want, and be firm with ourselves even when we feel frightened and small.

2. Avoid excessive self-disclosure early in therapy. Self-disclosure in the early phases of treatment tends to provide the client with a distraction from themselves. There is the risk that the client may overidentify with the therapist and in doing so not identify themselves. Therapists may wish to examine their motives for self-disclosure; often it is a desire to facilitate the client trusting the therapist. It is the author's belief that trusting resulting from therapist disclosure may provide a false sense of security to the client and may in the long run impede the therapeutic process.

3. Watch for dissociation on the part of the client. Dissociation or "leaving one's self" is one of the most common defenses against shame and it often occurs "automatically" as the client starts to feel frightened, angry, hurt, or ashamed. Once the therapist recognizes and labels the dissociation the client can be taught to recognize it. This is necessary in teaching clients to "stay with themselves." Some indications of client dissociation are glazing of the eyes, flattening of vocal characteristics, looking away, a sudden change in the topic of discussion to something other than the client, and a marked discrepancy between the client's verbal and nonverbal communications. While dissociation is a chronic defense with shame-based clients, it must be supported before

"inviting the client back to the present." The dissociation may be utilized by the therapist; the client could be said to already be in a light trance and is generally highly receptive to techniques such as therapeutic storytelling and imbedded suggestions.

4. Remember to "check in" with the client frequently. On a regular basis, the author will ask the client, "Where are we?" "What's going on?" or "How are you feeling about this relationship?" The use of immediacy keeps the therapeutic relationship free of unresolved issues which may arise but not be verbalized to the therapist. This requires that clients develop the important skill of representing themselves in an intimate relationship. Often the client may feel shameful over what they are thinking or feeling in relation to the therapist and the decision is made to not verbalize it because it was "silly," "stupid," or "unimportant." It is critical that when the client talks, the therapist listen and respond nondefensively.

5. Make sure you and your client have realistic goals. Many clients wish to rid themselves of shame. While this is understandable it is also virtually impossible. The goal of working with shame is to come to terms with it, such that the experience of shame is not disabling. In other words the goal of working with shame is to teach clients to "make friends" with their shame and to learn to value it as a basic part of being human. The healthy sharing of one's experience of shame is clearly an invitation to intimacy. Thus, shame may be redefined as a truly intimate experience with one's self and with others should they choose to respond to the invitation.

CONCLUSION

While not all recovering alcoholics experience severe difficulties with shame, the problem is common enough that alcohol and drug abuse professionals should at least be able to identify and refer the client if they are unable to respond to the problem. This article has briefly described the therapeutic process and technique of healing internalized shame. The process of healing shame may occur in most therapeutic settings, including treatment programs, self-help groups, and out patient psychotherapy.

Working with severely internalized shame requires a high degree of clinical skill and sensitivity.

REFERENCES

Beahrs, John O. (1982). *Unity and Multiplicity: Multilevel Consciousness to Self in Hypnosis, Psychiatric Disorder and Mental Health*, New York: Brunner/Mazel.

Fischer, B. (1986). The Dynamics and Healing of Shame; educational audiotape. Fieri Systems: P.O. Box 300036, Minneapolis, Minnesota.

Kaufman, Gershen (1985). *Shame: The Power of Caring* (revised edition). Cambridge, MA: Schenkman Publishing Company.

Kaufman, Gershen (1983). *The Dynamics of Power: Building A Competent Self*. Cambridge, MA: Schenkman Publishing Company.

Larsen, Earnie (1985). *Stage II Recovery: Life Beyond Addiction*. Minneapolis: Winston Press.

Miller, Alice (1981). *The Drama of the Gifted Child*. (R. Ward, Trans.). New York: Basic Books.

Schneider, Carl D. (1977). *Shame, Exposure, and Privacy*. Boston: Beacon Press.

Creative Approaches to Shame and Guilt: Helping the Adult Child of an Alcoholic

Patricia S. Potter-Efron, BA, CAC

SUMMARY. Shame and guilt are feeling experiences which powerfully affect adult children of alcoholics. Definitions of shame and guilt are provided, and several concrete methods described for the treatment of each in adult children from chemically dependent families. These techniques include those which enlarge the client's perspective, use resistive energy to move toward change, lead to greater self acceptance on the part of the client, and permit experimentation between therapist and client to locate a solution which is balanced and individualized for the client.

INTRODUCTION

Growing up in a family with chemical dependency can be very painful. The same is often true in any family with a history of long stress occasioned by mental or physical illness, or headed by a rigid, controlling person such as an adult child of an alcoholic. Parts of the pain experienced are visible to those who watch for them—for example, physical bruises, parental conflicts, a hungover person's irritability, a child remaining locked in his room away from his family, trying to appear invisible. Also often seen are the low self-esteem resulting from behavioral misconduct, rejection, or verbal abuse, the lack of easy relation-

Patricia S. Potter-Efron is affiliated with Personal Growth Services in Eau Claire, WI.

ship between the family and the external world, and the despair exhibited by some family members who only work, who withdraw, who pretend life is a joke, who cry with pain and depression, who may reject the world they were born into.

The greater pain lies below the surface, like the submerged portion of an iceberg — the frozen, numb, uncared for self.

Shame and guilt are common experiences of those who grow up in chemically dependent families, not just for the dependent but for each member of the family. To have an alcohol or other drug problem in the family is, in our society, to be shamed. Often family members who are not dependent are treated with pity, blame or hostility. Inescapably, feelings of being cheated and shamed come to the affected family member, along with guilt at having caused the problem or being unable to fix it.

Guilt and shame are both very powerful feelings and very painful ones. It is logical that chemically dependent persons and those who love them must develop strong defense systems to prevent despair and daily embarrassment; strong defenses are needed to hold family members together in spite of their pain. Without these systems of defense, individuals and families would find it hard to survive. Some of these defenses are denial, justification, control, dissociation, and the development of additional compulsive behaviors in the members of the family. These defenses develop over years of habitual responses to pain.

It is not a surprise, then, that when a counselor approaches the issue of chemical dependency, affected family members may deny the issue or protect the chemically dependent person. The counselor may be asking the family to open a wound which has already acquired scar tissue, and to be vulnerable all over again in a manner which has brought them shame or guilt before. The family in equilibrium with a using dependent has come to depend on the chemical dependency to provide a paradoxical but stable "background" to that family's everyday activities. To confront the family with the need to deal with chemical dependency is to trigger just the shame and guilt which has been defended against; the family member is being asked to examine his life and relationships in the harsh light of reality, without the best defenses he has developed to keep the pain out.

In this paper I will focus specifically on the treatment of shame and guilt with adult children of alcoholics. It is important to recognize, however, that adult children include many persons currently involved in a painful or chemically dependent family system with a spouse or child, sister or brother, as well as those who have not forgotten the pain of their relationship to their parents. For the purposes of this paper, an "adult child" will be defined as a current adult who has experienced long-term stress in his family of origin related to the chemical dependency of his parents or grandparents, and who is currently having difficulty maintaining optimum functioning in his present life.

DEFINITIONS OF GUILT AND SHAME

Guilt and shame are concepts which need to be briefly outlined here. The reader is referred to a more complete discussion in the first article of this volume (Potter-Efron, 1987).

In this article I will view guilt as a feeling response to violation of one's own values and societal values which have been internalized. Guilt is a failure or contemplated failure in the arena of behavior, a fault of doing. Shame, on the other hand, is a perceived failure of the self, a defectiveness exposed to the world. It is a failure of being, growing from the internalized self-concept on not being good or good enough. Shame is the sense that one is exposed to the world and seen a fraud.

It is true that shame and guilt have some positive functions. If I feel guilty when I lie, I may become more truthful and thus respect myself more. And shame may make me modest and more industrious so that I can meet my values more completely.

But adult children of alcoholics have learned the pain of shame and of guilt in a less functional manner. They have learned to be ashamed of themselves by association with their families, learned to see themselves as also guilty by association. Some of the most difficult issues for an adult child to resolve are guilt and responsibility issues, and the management of shame. The most persistent guilt issues are often those which are least rational and for which the individual cannot atone, not even by "making amends" as directed in the AA/Alanon twelve step programs (*Twelve Steps*, 1952). The most problematical shame issues are those which strongly affect identity and compassion for the self—a kind of compassion the adult child has likely never seen, and certainly not mastered. These guilt and shame issues are difficult to assess and to treat in a manner which allows a person to maintain self-forgiveness, forgiveness of others and a healthy sense of self over time.

Guilt and shame are both generated in the chemically dependent family in order to distribute the pain, and in such a manner as to support the addiction. They can be part of the defensive system of the family, strong bulwarks in supporting denial. (Wegscheider, 1979).

Additionally, shame especially can be triggered by very small events, ones which appear to be innocuous to the outside observer. A particular word, image or tone of voice, a small blemish, a slight challenge to the self which is taken personally can set up a strongly learned but inappropriate response which can lead such clients to become angry, guilty, ashamed, aggressive, or withdrawn in the therapeutic relationship, as well as in life in general. This may lead to clients dropping out of therapy, relapsing, returning to an older status quo, or raging at the therapist while addressing issues of shame and guilt.

APPROACHES TO BE USED

In the body of this article I will discuss general conditions important to dealing with therapeutic issues of shame and guilt. Following that, I will divide concerns into two categories: methods for dealing with shame and techniques for dealing with guilt. Some of the approaches discussed will be familiar to those working in the substance abuse field, and others are more unconventional. The latter have been developed to meet the special needs of adult children of alcoholics.

The criteria for including a technique in this paper are as follows: (1) the method alters or enlarges the perspective of the client; (2) the method allows resistive energy to be spent in healthy movement toward change rather than in the maintenance of the present problem; (3) the method makes a strong impact on the client's self-image, moving the person away from self-hatred and towards self-acceptance; and (4) it permits the client and therapist to experiment to find a balanced response to the client's needs and problems.

GENERAL CONDITIONS
OF THE THERAPEUTIC RELATIONSHIP

There are certain general conditions which must be met in the therapeutic setting to allow for effective intervention in the area of shame and guilt. The first and most important requirement is that the therapist exhibit and experience a sense of unconditional positive regard toward the client who will be dealing with problems of shame and guilt. This unconditional positive regard should be established from the first meeting, and reaffirmed in each session. If the therapist is not able to extend this to a particular client, the client should be referred elsewhere.

It is also imperative that the client be respected. It is important to remember that the adult child has grown up and may still be engaged in a family system which demands adherence to the rules, "Don't talk," "Don't trust" and "don't feel." (Black, 1982). For many, their exposure to chemical dependency intervention and treatment or to outpatient therapy will be the first relationship they have developed which specifically breaks these family rules. It is important the client hear that his discomfort and reluctance is normal and will be respected, even though he is encouraged to try new behavior.

When dealing with an adult child with strong shame and guilt issues, it is also important to deal with fear of abandonment and rejection right away. Gershen Kaufman points out that neglect and rejection are shame-producing events (Kaufman, 1980). The adult child has often been actually abandoned or neglected physically or emotionally, producing feelings of not being good, significant, or lovable. It is often relevant to find out how the client is viewing the therapist, and how they think the therapist might hurt them, if such an unlikely event were to occur. This provides the client the opportunity to immediately express fears or needs in a context which is serious but still somewhat superficial.

Simple sharing of shame-based experience is powerful and basic work. Problems are lighter when shared, and shame is less strong once an issue is exposed and the shamed person survives the exposure. Shame can be a consuming experience, the result of which are feelings of defectiveness, inadequacy, or self-hatred. These feelings have occasioned strong attempts to avoid the shame and when internalized and generalized present as an inability to like, respect or care for oneself (Kaufman, 1980). Such feelings can also result in a self-concept which is oppositional to anyone else who is ready and willing to care for the self. This being so, it is especially important to acknowledge the shame and the pain, and to provide the client with an opportunity to perceive himself in a new way. Some adult children will need extended outpatient treatment to make progress in the area of self-esteem.

CREATIVE METHODS FOR DEALING WITH SHAME

I want to suggest here that certain creative techniques for the treatment of the shamed person are useful in dealing with profound shame experiences. These methods are at times preferable to simply confronting the shameful event. Methods I will address here include the following: (1) mirror work; (2) use of stuffed animals and dolls; (3) use of concrete objects; (4) clay work; and (5) drawing and visualization.

Mirror Work

Shame presents itself as if it were a stain (Potter-Efron, 1987), and as with the anorexic who looks at herself in the mirror and sees herself as fat, adult children with a history of verbal, emotional and/or physical abuse may see themselves as ugly, or even as persons who literally cannot look themselves in the eye. While practicing looking in the mirror may seem silly, mirror work is an effective tool for treating shame which exhibits itself in this manner. In mirror work it is essential to regard the assignment as acceptance of and intimate contact with oneself, not others. The therapist should be prepared to demonstrate or model the assignment of affirming oneself in a mirror, and to disclose how she herself feels doing this assignment. Because many adult children see themselves as different from other people (Woititz), self-disclosure will help in binding the client and therapist into a real world which they can share together.

Mirror work is an opportunity to reinforce that loving and appreciating the self is a crucial part of recovery from chemically affected living. The therapist can also point out that we treat ourselves as others have treated us (Kaufman, 1980), and that the adult child may have been treated with contempt, treated with dislike, or taught to treat himself with rejection. Intervention such as this may stimulate the client to remember and to share painful and shame-filled memories with the therapist. It is a major change to have practice in appreciating the self and it combats the negative self-image of the shamed person.

Use of Stuffed Animals and Dolls

There are many possible reasons to employ therapy aids such as stuffed animals; one of the best may be that holding something soft, real, and unrejecting is healing for the person whose environment has been harsh, confusing and abusive. The criteria for the physical object — in this case a doll or stuffed animal — is that it be an external model which can be accepted by the client as representing himself, or a part of himself which he may have lost.

The adult child in therapy has a history of many rejections and neglects. A common problem produced by the stress and shame in the chemically dependent family is that the adult child has often given up being "childish" at an early age, or has been restricted to very specific roles as a child. In addition to these deprivations, inconsistency and abuse have taken their toll. As Kaufman points out (Kaufman, 1980), to be ignored, ridiculed or simply treated with contempt is unambivalent rejection. The child's needs and wants become unimportant distractions in the chemically dependent family; many adult children have traumatic memories of the child they were at a young age. Others have none at all.

In addressing this loss of childhood or lack of childhood memories, it is a good idea to assign the adult child client to buy a stuffed animal for himself. Instructions should be that it be a stuffed animal of the same "gender" as its owner (many women have only had "male" stuffed animals), and that this animal or doll in particular is only for its purchaser and cannot be given to his children. Even "macho" males need not be excluded from this assignment—some men compromise by buying animal hand puppets, thus retaining a sense of control over their masculinity.

One simple way of finding relevant information about shame is to have the client relax and travel back to crucial childhood times. As memories are found and shared, the old "sad" and "bad" feelings well up. This is the point in the interaction between therapist and client where the interpersonal bridge (Kaufman, 1980) is most easily broken, a point at which the client ceases eye contact, looks down, and withdraws from the therapist just as a shamed person looks at the floor and draws back, unable to look at the shaming parents. This is precisely the moment when a doll or stuffed animal can maintain the interpersonal bridge between therapist and client by giving the client a way in which to have self-nurturing experience with himself. A doll can be given into the person's arms and the person asked to focus on the child he remembers. The client is asked to hold the child, and to comfort that child in the present; a parallel is teaching a parent to hold his newborn child. Use of stuffed animals is a way of reestablishing the link between the adult and the child he carries within himself (Whitfield, 1986), who is ashamed and afraid of the world. That relationship having been reestablished, the individual is no longer so totally dependent on the therapist for love of the shamed self, and can begin to be more compassionate and less self-hating with himself.

Dean is a family "hero" who has worked all his life for approval, and is never "good enough." No matter how well Dean does, he feels that he is deficient due to his strong need for approval and his long-term relationship with family shame. Dean chose to buy himself a stuffed penguin which represents a comic strip penguin who is the child of a herring juice addicted mother. This penguin was identified in the comic strip as a "flightless waterfowl" (Breathed, 1985), and Dean stated that that is exactly how he feels about himself. Initially Dean made jokes about himself and his inadequacies by pointing to his penguin. But in a short time he has become able to hold and hug that part of himself during therapy, and to accept the needs it represents—the need for approval, caring, and just plain love for who he is. He has chosen to sleep with the animal and not be embarrassed in front of his wife. In fact he took his wife shopping to buy her own stuffed animal. As he has allowed himself to meet some needs for touch, holding, and caring by doing those very things to his penguin, he has become more able to both accept and to express his real self to his family. He has become able to share his caring and his frustration with his alcoholic parents and to recognize that he needs to approve of himself instead of depending on them for approval he will never receive. He has become able to be playful with his wife and children, something he had not been able to unbend enough to do in the past. As Dean accepts himself as a "flightless waterfowl," he is becoming more successful in the relationships in his life, and less dependent on his family of origin for emotional survival. He is becoming more able to detach from the alcoholic members of his family; he is becoming a whole person and less a "mannequin," his own word for his codependent self.

Use of Concrete Objects

Concrete objects provide another powerful method for helping a person look at himself and handle the dissociative effects of shame and rejection in his life. This is particularly true for persons who are verbally limited, or limited in expression of feelings by strong rage or oppositional responses toward shame. A concrete object can be accepted into the hand or even the heart without the words that raise defenses and fears of shameful experience. To pick up a rock, a shell, a nested doll, a statuette, a beautiful object or even a discarded object is a physical event which can be reversed, and a physical act which only rarely leads to strong shame responses. To explore a physical object and notice how it is like you, is an adventure in curiosity and identification which temporarily can remove characteristic defenses against shame and provide a new way to look at one's self-image. It can also allow a person to look at his responses to abuse without triggering the deep shame which makes the pain intolerable, and necessitates explosion or dissociation. In other words, an individual can explore his responses to his life situation in a less threatening manner than usual, and in a manner which can also lead to an exploration of his strengths.

Concrete objects which I use are from two categories: objects with flaws and objects with special qualities. Objects with flaws include such things as a bird with one wing, a shell with barnacles on it, a "Dad's" root beer bottle which has been distorted by being heated and cooled, and a torn picture. Objects with special qualities include such things as a geode, a funerary supply bottle, an empty alcohol bottle, and a perpetual motion machine.

Most often I ask the adult child client to look over a small array of concrete objects with the instruction that he should allow an object to *choose him,* or with instructions to choose an object which repeatedly calls itself to his attention. I then give one of the following instructions:

1. Take this object everywhere with you, and allow it to give you the message it holds for you;
2. Take this object home and find out what it needs. As far as you can, satisfy its needs, and then bring it back here;
3. Tell me how this object is like you. Then take it with you this week and see if you notice any other ways it is like you.

Two examples of adult children's work with objects are below.

Jim was the child of two alcoholics and was himself in treatment. He was drawn to a small wooden heart with an empty space inside which he stated was just as empty as he was. I assigned him to put objects relating to his empty heart inside, whether he did so by placing an actual object there or by writing notes on paper and putting them into the "emptiness." At the end of a week Jim had gathered pictures from his children, a poem about sobriety, a ring linking himself to his wife, and several other things. At the end of the week Jim was aware that his heart was full rather than empty, and had gained the motivation to stay in treatment.

Objects with special qualities are particularly useful in helping adult children who have negative self-images resulting from being shamed; through objects with special qualities it is possible to aid these clients in recognizing and taking pride in their strengths as well as in working through shame.

Dick came to me first in aftercare, because he was an adult child of an alcoholic and had personality difficulties which made him inappropriate for aftercare group placement. It was clear that without some work on his shame he would be unable to stay sober for long. In fact, he had two lapses during his first six weeks of aftercare. Dick was oppositional, and determined to show he was not worth anything. Finally I asked Dick to choose an object to work with. His first response was to pick up an object that looked to him like a big, ugly rock. However, it was a geode, rough on the outside, but with agate lines and soft purple crystals hidden in the underside. We discussed how Dick was similar to the rough exterior of the rock, and how both had been, in a way, forged by fire. I asked Dick to simply sit with the rock for ten minutes before bed every night, and he did do this for one month. Then, on his own, Dick cleaned both sides of the geode carefully with a toothbrush, and brought it back shimmering with cleanliness and beauty. Shortly thereafter his behavior with his wife and children began to change. He became less demanding and able to show them his love more. When Dick got in trouble for fighting at work, he took the rock home with him again for two weeks. This time his behavior changed very quickly as he refused to allow other workers' shaming and ridicule touch him. He simply behaved as if they had no power over him, like a "rock." When he returned the geode it was with the understanding that he could use it again if he needed it. When he was put into a therapy group, he used the geode to introduce himself. Dick is continuing in group and jokes about keeping the geode the next time he uses it. Really Dick is considering *keeping himself* now that he is experiencing pride in himself instead of shame.

The special qualities of the geode have helped Dick and others similar to him to find special qualities in themselves, and to locate strength which they have forgotten or not discovered. Such use of concrete objects aids clients in seeing, feeling, identifying and touching parts of themselves which they cannot or will not share in words and in usual therapeutic concepts.

Working with Clay

I have mentioned the importance of nonverbal methods already. Another important medium which allows for both verbal explanation and nonverbal power and representation of shame-related material is clay. Clay is an especially effective medium where the client has suffered abuse that gives rise to shame, at the hands of others. Persons who have been victims of severe physical and emotional abuse, and especially those who have been victims of sexual abuse, are good candidates for working through shame in the medium of clay.

Certain qualities of clay support and encourage shame-related feelings within a context where the client is also allowed some control over what he produces. The ability to control what he makes of the clay is a vital kind of control for the person who has experienced humiliation; in fact, a client may deal with shame-based and crucial material more readily when he feels he has control. The quality and texture of the clay itself may bring up old shame material which results in a client's talking about getting his hands "dirty." The nature of the medium is also such that aggression is needed to mold it. Thus, when sensations of shame and disgust occur, the client is encouraged by the clay itself to use the fight response rather than a flight response. Clay as a medium of expression additionally demands and provides a sense of momentum in working it, and aids the client to cross the bridge of self-consciousness and self-hatred in externalizing painful feelings. The physical quality of the clay keeps the client in touch with himself and enables him to feel in charge, at the same time making it harder for the client to censor himself and his expression. It is particularly applicable in working with shame because it provides a medium for the expression of shame and its attendant defense, rage.

Clay gives the client a sense that he can unmake what he has made, and in a way destroy the very thing which hurts him so much. This being so, clay is a good intervention for persons who have dissociated from pain through becoming numb, or who live in another world. Clay supplies a grounding in this world, which alleviates part of the pain of expression. It is common to see regressive figures represented in the clay without the client himself regressing during the session. The regressive posture represented in the clay allows a client to share his painful and ashamed inner self without having to become a rageful or hurt two-year-old.

Dan was an adult child of an alcoholic married to another adult child who had serious trouble communicating and was very rejecting. Dan was often manipulative in the relationship in order to meet his needs. When he was asked to represent his past, he made a lifelike male sitting bent in shame and covering his genitals. As Dan spoke to me about his shame and rejection by his alcoholic and contemptuous mother, and his angry wife, he also spoke to himself through the clay. Each week he straightened the bent figure a little until after four weeks the clay man was sitting upright and molding some clay in his own hands. As he continued to work, Dan made a figure of himself portaging a canoe alone, and then one of himself and his wife sitting and paddling a canoe together, This expressed Dan's desire for a closer relationship, and his wife responded by agreeing to take a substantial canoe trip with him.

Visualizing the Self

As there are instances and persons for whom the experience of shame must be allowed so that it can be worked through, there are other more fragile individuals who need to have access to a way of working through shame without strong feelings being triggered. These may include those who have come to see their own needs as alien and monstrous, and who have come to feel evil and inhuman when experiencing themselves as needing. Also included are those who cannot tolerate the experience of shame because they are currently in a crisis which calls for them to stay in control.

Visualization plays an important role in this process, allowing a client to explore the self as it now is, in a metaphorical manner. This may allow clients to see parts of themselves they may have buried without raising the feelings of terror and shame which they avoid with such necessity.

Visualization techniques which are helpful in the treatment of shame and guilt are as follows:

1. Visualizing the client's own heart, how it looks and feels, and providing active intervention where necessary (for example, visualizing a friendly campfire warming up the icy blue heart of a shamed, numb person).
2. Visualization of the self at a specific age standing near a childhood home, and seeing the client's own adult self intervening to rescue the child if danger appears.
3. Visualizing the child within the adult self, and having the child tell the present adult what it needs.
4. Visualizing being Alice in Wonderland or the white rabbit going down the rabbit hole, and looking at what goes on in the client in a metaphorical way.
5. Visualizing a light behind the client's eyes, and having it float slowly down into the inner darkness, to light up what exists inside.

GUILT IN ADULT CHILDREN OF ALCOHOLICS

Members of chemically dependent families engage in strongly guilt-generating behaviors including a focus on maintaining personal control at all times, penalties for even thinking about transgressions, blaming without explaining, and an emphasis on the responsibility for all family behavior being given to each individual.

Behaviors such as these create an enlargement of responsibility for the adult child—a responsibility which permeates his life so that even small events may be responded to with inordinate guilt. Guilt rises even when the individual could not have changed and cannot make amends for the events. This guilt contributes to the massive resentment which many adult children possess under the veneer of being overly responsible or disengaged from the family.

Straightforward incidents of guilt can most often be treated by discussing the situation and helping the adult child identify and change a problematical behavior, or by helping the adult child to recognize that he can make current amends for transgressions in the past.

However, some adult children appear to cling to their guilt. The motivational sources for this clinging may be complex. In some cases feeling guilty is more acceptable than owning that the adult child himself has had no power over the behavior of members of his family. To be helpless in the face of such a painful problem as chemical dependency may deeply frighten a person, and need to be denied. Some adult children cling to guilt at having been abused less than other members of the family. Others seem to cling to guilt as an alternative to allowing themselves to express anger and resentment which would not be acceptable in the family. In such cases the guilt (and the hidden resentments that occur with it) often powers compulsive behaviors which also help to avoid feelings. In some instances a person will develop a lifestyle which itself rests upon the continuance and renewed creation of guilt in the self and the family. When this occurs, it is common to find the guilty and resentful person taking the stance of a martyr — a self-punishing and all-sacrificing role accompanied by a complaining self-righteousness.

CREATIVE METHODS FOR DEALING WITH GUILT

These occurrences of guilt can be dealt with creatively in substance abuse therapy. Among the most effective tactics I have found are the following: (1) stealing responsibility; (2) the guilt contest; and (3) marbles and potatoes.

Stealing Responsibility

The simplest of these techniques is to reframe the guilty, enabling person in the family as the person who "robs" other family members of their rightful responsibilities. When the guilty person takes on jobs for others, takes emotional responsibility for bygone events due to a current crisis, or when they make excuses for the irresponsibility of other members of the family, it is helpful to state explicitly that these are the particular behaviors with which the enabler steals responsibility which belongs to others. The implications are that in their guilty behavior they unwittingly play the part of a thief in which they violate other people's rights to be responsible. To be violating another's rights is a very difficult position for an already guilty, self-righteous person to be in.

Clearly, the enabling adult child must find out how to behave "better" so he will feel less guilty.

As he learns to behave better by being less over-responsible, he experiences the alleviation of guilt for stealing. A client who is feeling guilty does not wish the added burden of being a "thief" added to his life. When he accepts this reframing of his behavior, he is often able to let go of irrational guilt and of responsibilities he has taken since childhood. And sometimes the changing of just one key person's behavior will lead to lasting change within the family circle.

The Guilt Contest

In group therapy with adult children, it is common to have persons who are controlling and guilty reinforce each other. While group members may talk about "letting go," they continue to lament the fact that they still feel guilty about other people's behavior as well as their own. Then commonly say that they do not know how to change these attitudes. Teaching and supporting detachment is difficult in a group with four or five of these overly responsible individuals. One intervention which is powerful enough to alter the behavior of more than one of these adult children at a time is the "guilt contest."

The idea is to have a 'contest' to see who is the most guilty party among group members. Most group members will feel a bit ambivalent, but those asked to join with usually do so. It is common in this contest/exercise for participants to begin with low level statements of "I feel guilty when my house isn't clean," and then move into a more powerful phase. The group leader may have to gently reiterate instructions. Often group members will discuss feeling guilty taking time in group, feeling guilty about feeling guilty, and feeling guilty for not being able to come up with statements about what they feel guilty about. When encouraged to continue and to make this contest an important way for themselves to grow, the group will move to the next phase. This is composed ordinarily of quiet, strong statements of things they feel guilty about in regard to alcoholism and other important areas of their lives. Tears and anger may be exhibited. It is important to designate all participants in the guilt "contest" as winners who have explored themselves in a significant way, and not to vote on who won or lost.

Marbles and Potatoes

Marbles and potatoes is an assignment which can be given either to a single member of a group or to an adult child in individual therapy. I prefer to use it in individual sessions to limit self-consciousness. This is an especially powerful technique for those who are guilty and preoccupied, continually worrying about others in their lives, and who use their guilt to distract themselves from anger and resentment they fear to express.

The technique is very simple. A person is given twenty marbles of any type. He is asked to list his guilt feelings out loud, and to put one marble aside for each thing he is feeling guilty about. When this has been completed, the therapist removes the extra marbles and counts those representing guilt feelings. The client is then assigned to stop at a grocery store on the way home, and to buy one potato fist-sized or larger, for each guilt feeling he has listed. He is told that he may put these potatoes in any kind of container he chooses, but he must carry them with him everywhere he goes until the next therapy session (one week is optimal timing). He is assigned to bring his potatoes to the next therapy session, and during that appointment he is encouraged to deal with his resentments about the "guilty" potatoes. I have found it best to deal with guilts/resentments one at a time and to extend the assignment of carrying the rest of the potatoes which have not been dealt with into subsequent weeks. Then, when the adult child is avoidant and fails to deal with a powerful feeling (represented by a potato), often the potato itself will sprout and/or get slightly rotten. It is at this point in time that the therapist and the client (who by now is getting very tired of carrying potatoes) can look at the overall effects and consequences that guilt and preoccupation have had on the client's life. This includes looking at guilty and resentful feelings that developed in the family of origin, are very old, and are quite comparable to rotten potatoes.

CONCLUSION

Guilt and shame are profound experiences of children of alcoholics and may affect their ability to function as mature adults. In this article creative methods of treating guilt and shame have been presented as guides and experiments for other practitioners to use.

REFERENCES

Black, Claudia, *It Will Never Happen To Me*. Denver, Colorado: M.A.C. Printing and Publishing, 1982.

Breathed, Burke, "Bloom County" cartoons, 1985.

Cermak, Timmen, *A Primer on Adult Children of Alcoholics*. Pompano Beach, Florida: Health Communications. 1985.

Forrest, Gary, *Alcoholism, Narcissism and Psychopathology*. Springfield, Illinois: Charles Thomas Publishing, 1983.

Fromm, Erich, *The Art of Loving*. New York: Harper and Row, 1956.

Kaufman, Gershen, *Shame: The Power of Caring*. Cambridge, Massachusetts: Schenkman, 1980.

Kurtz, Ernest, *Shame and Guilt: Characteristics of the Dependency Cycle*. Center City: Hazelden Press, 1981.

Ramsey, Edward, *Handbook for a Chemical Abuser and Those Concerned*. Eau Claire, Wisconsin: Bartingale Press, 1984.

Twelve Steps and Twelve Traditions. New York: Alcoholics Anonymous World Service Organization, 1952.

Wegscheider, Don, *If Only My Family Understood Me . . .* Minneapolis, Minnesota: Comp Care Publications, 1979.

Wegscheider, Sharon, *Another Chance*. Palo Alto: Science and Behavior Books, 1981.

Whitefield, Charles L., *Healing the Child Within*. Baltimore, Maryland: The Resource Group, 1986.

Woititz, Janet Geringer, *Adult Children of Alcoholics*. Pompano Beach, Florida: Health Communications, 1983.

Woititz, Janet Geringer, *Struggle for . . . Intimacy*. Pompano Beach, Florida: Health Communications, 1985.

Zinker, Joseph, *Creative Process in Gestalt Therapy*. New York: Brunner/Mazel, 1977.

Rekindled Spirit of a Child: Intervention Strategies for Shame with Elementary Age Children of Alcoholics

Barbara Naiditch

SUMMARY. The author discusses the shaming effects that occur among children who are raised in chemically dependent families. Therapeutic techniques are provided to help children gain greater self-esteem and coping mechanisms while living in this situation.

Shame strongly affects alcoholics and their families. Because of their shame, family members may attempt to cover their disgrace both from others and themselves, adding to the strength of denial in these families. Shame keeps families from seeking help, destroys self-esteem, and produces destructive secrets that cannot heal. When children are born into an alcoholic family system, their first developmental task is to decide how much they can trust their parents. These children also begin to decide how likeable, lovable, and capable they are depending on the attention they receive.

Children need to be consciously wanted. The parent or parents must be available emotionally and physically for the child so the child's needs can be met and trust developed. In alcoholic family systems this trust usually is not developed. The first developmental task is not completed and thus must be redone for a person to move on developmentally in their life cycle and in recovery.

By using Erickson's stages of Growth and Pamela Levin's Af-

Barbara Naiditch is Co-Director of Children Are People, Inc., in St. Paul, MN.

firmational Stages of Development, I will show how shame develops in a child born into an alcoholic family system as contrasted to a functional family system. Then, this paper will explain four intervention strategies that can help relieve shame for elementary age children of alcoholics: the Children Are People Support Group Model, play, affirmations and the 12 step program.

CHEMICALLY DEPENDENT FAMILY SYSTEMS AND EFFECTS ON THE DEVELOPMENT OF SHAME

Self-esteem is a family affair (Clark). The very first experiences children have lead to decisions about how likeable, capable and loveable they are. Depending on the touch received, wordless messages perceived, words spoken to them, and positive messages given out, children make decisions on their own self-esteem (Briggs). In order for a real, mutual relationship between child and parent to develop properly, the following conditions are necessary: the child must be consciously wanted and the parent must be able to be there emotionally for the child to meet his or her core needs and not the reverse (Kaufman). Respectful family systems see self and members as being related and part of the universe and implies a place to belong.

Relationships have substance and resilience. People tend to talk openly with one another about their lives rather than manage their relationships with secrets. Pain doesn't have to be denied or judged (Fossom & Mason). Thus, children from these families are relatively shame free.

What are the characteristics of a family affected by parental alcoholism? The family atmosphere is characterized by chaos and unpredictability. There is an inconsistency of behavioral expectations and limits, physical and emotional care and responsiveness to communication and interactions (Fox).

In many alcoholic families the alcoholism is a major secret and this secret is the major focus around which the family becomes organized. The alcoholic family becomes increasingly isolated and defensive. In this atmosphere, childhood is short of nonexistent. The child learns to manage the actions of others, always attempting to ward off disaster. The child also learns to parcel out feelings so as to avoid upsetting the alcoholic or being held responsible for precipitating a drinking bout. Thus the child's feelings, needs and behaviors are dictated by the state of the alcoholic at any given time in the drinking cycle (Beletsis and Brown).

When a child fails to experience that a parent wants a relationship with him or her as a separate individual, shame most often results. It is the parent's actions rather than words which convince the child that he/she counts as a person in his/her own right. Shame can also be rooted in a parent looking to the child to make up for the parent's deficiencies or to live out the parent's dreams as though the child were an extension of the self of the parent. When the parent does not parent the child and when the parent is not there emotionally, the child becomes entangled in a web of uncertainty. The conditions for basic security are absent and the child will come to feel unwanted in some fundamental sense. If this pattern of rejection persists over time the child will come to feel that he/she is lacking in some fundamental way — emptiness in the soul emerges.

Another problem for children in the chemically dependent family is that they may believe they are the cause for the alcoholic parent's drinking. Children need to know they don't cause alcoholism, and it is not their behavior which causes a parent to continue drinking alcoholically. Children need to be reassured that even if they behave in a way which upsets a parent, that their parent has many choices other than drinking to handle the situation. Children also may feel guilty for having conflicting feelings of love and hate for the alcoholic or non-alcoholic parent (Black).

Children who live in actively using alcoholic homes continue to have losses. The losses they experience are the following: loss of safety, vague boundaries, loss of friendships, loss of whole experiences, loss of memories, loss of learning to play, loss of positive rewards, loss of own needs, loss of right to nurture, and loss of childhood (Middleton-Moz).

Shame plays a major role in the emotional condition of depressed people. Depressed children are affected with an attributional style that interprets bad events as resulting from their own personal deficiencies. This attributional style may be considered to reflect chronic low self-esteem or chronic shame.

Children of alcoholics often have personality disturbances manifested by signs of hostility, impulsiveness, depression and sexual confusion. The depression in this case is the result of a basic feeling of anxiety and may surface as feelings of irritability or worthlessness, fear of the future, poor appetite, insomnia or even suicide attempts (Sloboda).

For children of alcoholics, the embarrassment of living in an alcoholic home is often intense because the stigma attached to drunkenness is so powerful. When young people are ashamed of their parents every day the shame can spread to a feeling of being ashamed of themselves. This shame can go on to become self-hatred which hinders the individual from constant close relationships (Seixas). Shame generated by alcoholic parents is devastating to the child because the child subscribes to the parents' attitudes. Its effects will continue to distort the daily living of the child unless there is an intervention process.

SHAME GENERATING MESSAGES
IN CHEMICALLY DEPENDENT FAMILIES

In order to begin to repair the shame within a child, one must understand the stages of development of children in a healthy vs. a chemically dependent family system. According to Pamela Levin (Levin), each stage of the developmental cycle has its own affirming messages that help children move from one stage of development to the next. These positive messages nurture self-esteem positive growth and positive direction. Negative messages discount the child's identity.

Different messages are needed at each stage of the child's development. I will address the following stages which I have combined and summarized from the works of Erickson, Levin and Brown and Beletsis.

Trust: Ages Birth-5
Evaluation: Ages 6-12
Transition: Ages 12-18
Recycling: Ages 18- +

TRUST: (0-5 years) For the very young child, the development of trust is crucial. The development of trust is an ongoing process and is the necessary cornerstone for a healthy attitude toward self and others in interpersonal relationships (Brown & Beletsis).

In a family where either parent is alcoholic, the trust relationship will be impaired. The spouse may be preoccupied with problems in the relationship and the focus of both parents will either be toward the alcoholic or toward alcohol. The result is psychological abandonment of the child or inadequate and inconsistent caretaking. This is the beginning of shame development. Fueled by unmet needs, the child of an alcoholic remains focused on the parent and cannot experience awareness of self as a distinct person. Thus, development of autonomy is impaired. This is the perfect breeding ground for shame.

Children feel like something is wrong with them because no one will totally take care of them. The messages that children need to complete this developmental stage include the following: "I'm glad you are here," "You have every right to be here," "Your needs are ok," "I'm glad you are a boy," "I'm glad you are a girl," "You don't have to take care of adults" and "You can express your feelings straight" (Levin & Clarke).

The second stage of development is one of *EVALUATION* (ages 6-12). During this stage, children are learning how to do things their own way and to develop opinions and thinking skills. If this stage is not appropriately worked through, children will have a difficult time making decisions, expressing opinions and standing up for themselves.

In an alcoholic family system, children are many times reprimanded for their own opinions, rarely given direct positive attention, and responded to in either an angry or bothersome manner on part of the parents. If the child doesn't receive personal acknowledgement they learn to manipulate negatively to receive recognition. Most of the attention of the adults is either on the alcohol or on the alcoholic.

The following developmental messages are needed for children to complete this stage of development: "You can trust your feelings to guide you," "You can do it your way," "It's ok to disagree," and "You don't have to suffer to get what you need" (Levin and Clarke).

The third stage is one of *TRANSITIONS* (ages 13-18). This is a stage of working through old problems, separating from parents and finding a place among grownups. This stage is crucial in teaching children how to work through unhealthy relationships.

During this stage the child of an alcoholic is in a double bind. The driving need to deny feelings and needs is a denial of self and an avoidance of having an independent identity. The role reversals which have taken place since early childhood leave the child defended against being a dependent child and defended against being an adult parent to the out-of-control alcoholic. The resolution may be an adolescent identity as a pseudo-adult, feeling helpless and frightened, appearing overly mature and capable, striving for control (Beletsis & Brown).

The messages needed to complete this stage of development for the adolescent are as follows: "It's ok to know who you are," "You are welcome to come home again," "You can be a sexual person and still have needs," and "You are loved."

The final stage is called *RECYCLING* (ages 18 through adulthood). This is a period of time that adults can work on changing the negative messages they received (Levin). During this stage, reclaiming and rebuilding power is the main task. This is the stage that gives people permission to bring their child traits out of hiding — the little child that disappeared by having to grow up too fast to manage the actions of others. Also during this stage, adults can have a chance to identify the missing developmental messages that were not reinforced and a chance to reexperience them.

The reinforcement of shame continues through each stage of development in the alcoholic family system. A young child experiences shame as abandonment especially when he/she doesn't feel free to be dependent on parents or other adults for comfort, for needs, and for touch. Shame blocks the autonomy that is crucial to breaking co-dependent behavior. During the evaluation stage of development (ages 6-12) many children feel inadequate and starved for recognition. They take on defenses that protect their shame — perfectionism, control, rage, striving for power, transferring of blame, and internal withdrawal (Kaufman). During adolescence, shame will continue when individual identity is blocked. Understanding and delivering the key developmental messages to the child is a crucial vehicle for shame intervention by parents and other adults.

FOUR INTERVENTION TECHNIQUES TO HELP THE CHILD IN A CHEMICALLY DEPENDENT FAMILY WITH SHAME ISSUES

Validation of the Child Through Positive Interaction

Children of alcoholics need early intervention in healing shame. What needs to happen in approaching a shame-based child is open validation of his or her feelings. To validate feelings means to begin to build an interpersonal bridge. Building this bridge gradually allows the child to lessen the need for defending strategies and makes possible experiences of vulnerability and openness. Once built, this bridge between child and counselor needs to be maintained and thus becomes an ongoing process.

As this bridge becomes stronger, the child begins to develop a stronger identity based on three characteristics: affirming the self, finding a spiritual identity, and positive searching for wholeness and worth (Kaufman). The main task of a therapist then is to provide the environment to help children begin the process of building a strong identity as a means to the prevention of chemical dependency and to assist in the intervention of shame. Techniques useful for therapists to help build trust and a stronger identity in children are structured activities, direct listening skills and play.

Recognition of Powerlessness Over Another Person's Thoughts, Actions and Deeds: Step 1 of Twelve Step Recovery Program

Because shame strips children of the nutrients that are needed to be whole human beings (Stephanie K.) our task is to reeducate children, especially high risk children from chemically dependent families on step 1 of the 12 step program.

Role play is a powerful technique used to demonstrate Step 1. Children need to learn they didn't cause the alcoholism in their family, they can't cure it, yet they can cope with it. To demonstrate this concept, the following role play can be used: ask the children in the classroom to form one large circle. Choose four children to sit in the middle of one circle. Two children in the middle can represent alcohol and marijuana. Ask the children in the middle to pretend that they are having a party (they are happy, having fun, etc.) Ask the children on the outside of the circle to be sad and silent. Choose one person to go into the middle of the circle and join the "party." (The teacher now goes through the stages of addiction) The teacher emphasizes that this is an example of how people abuse chemicals. Remind the class that it is illegal for children to use alcohol or drugs without parental permission. (a) Ask the child (Johnny) to go back and join the outside circle. Explain that the people inside the circle represent drugs and Johnny has just learned that taking a chemical is fun and can make him feel better temporarily. (b) Ask Johnny to go into the middle again. Explain that this is the seeking stage. Johnny feels better when he is using drugs and looks forward to using drugs. Ask Johnny to go back to the circle and explain that at this stage he still has the choice not to use drugs. (c) Ask Johnny to go into the middle again. Explain that this is the loss of choice stage. Ask the children representing drugs to hold onto Johnny's arms and legs. Ask Johnny to try to rejoin the circle. He cannot — he has no choice — he must use drugs because now his body is controlled by the drug. Then ask the children if anyone made him use the drugs; they will visually see that they cannot push anyone to use drugs. They are powerless. The leader then stresses that they cannot cause dependency; they cannot cure dependency; they can learn to cope with this disease. (d) Ask the children representing chemicals to continue to hold onto Johnny's arms and legs. Ask Johnny to look sad. Explain to the children that the last stage of dependency produces *extremely* harmful consequences if the person does not get help: illness, trouble with the law, insanity, family problems . . . or even death. (Naiditch and Lerner).

Play

In order to combat shame children have to be taught how to play and become children again. Play allows children to work through painful emotional experiences. Children can recreate their experience of loss through play and get it out of their system especially when paired with parental comfort or another trusting adult. For children play is the language of their feelings. Adults use words—children use play. The purpose of play is to help rebuild or restore a relationship with the child.

When a therapist reintroduces a child to play he/she needs to be able to model playful behavior. To work with children and recreate a playful, humorous environment therapists would have had to recycle their first two stages of development in order to validate their internal childlike spirit. A therapist needs to model play visually. For instance, using imagination, fairy tales, physical activities (sports), and humor, can help a child feel more confident and trusting of the therapists. Children can then transfer this validation to their own personal life.

Another useful technique is to play "New Games" with a group of children. (New Games Foundation) New Games are emotionally and physically safe. All ages and sizes of children and adults can play. The games are played with mutual cooperation and are empowered by the players. These games can enhance a positive attitude toward play by their silliness.

The benefits for children are that the games increase participation, release tension, create playfulness, fun, build self-worth, celebrates life, physically release stress and assists with individual expression.

Support Groups

Support Groups for children of alcoholics are an important tool in the intervention of shame. Intervention refers to the attempt to help children comprehend both cognitively and affectively the real nature of family alcoholism and its effects on their feelings, attitudes and actions. Prior to intervention most children of alcoholics hide or deny the family secret or harmfully act out their confused feelings and emotionally isolate themselves from others. Intervention legitimizes their feelings and encourages them to develop new ways to express them (Deutsch, Dicicco & Mills). Children Are People, Inc. in St. Paul, Minnesota, has facilitated Support Groups for elementary age children of alcoholics for the past ten years. These groups gently confront the shame in the children by education, structure, play, affirmations and slogans. The children are taught how to protect themselves and recognize their own powerlessness over others.

Some of the goals of Support Group which confront shame issues with children of alcoholics are: (a) To teach children the following information about chemical dependency: They did not cause it — They cannot cure it — They can cope with it; (b) To teach children how to recognize their powerlessness over the alcoholic in their family; (c) To teach children how to recognize their powerlessness over other people's emotions and behaviors; (d) To build a sense of trust with adults through the counselors or facilitators who are consistent role models; and (e) To teach children how to identify and communicate feelings. These groups are run on eight week cycles so there is a beginning when new participants can join and a closure to evaluate the next step. Each week one topic is introduced along with a slogan to help reinforce the concept. The groups have two co-facilitators with twelve children. The manner in which shame is confronted in the group process can best be illustrated by briefly describing five topics: goal setting with child and parent, feelings, defenses, chemical dependency, specialness and family communication group.

The first week of group is a scheduled intake with parent and child. During this time goals are set with parent and child. The main objectives are: to teach *goal setting* as a self-esteem building tool, to focus attention onto themselves and their behaviors, to provide an opportunity to learn appropriate control, responsibility and accomplishment. Goal setting helps children have control over their own lives and develop autonomy. Goals are established by the children that are measurable and reachable. Completion of a goal helps a child feel successful and proud.

The next topic that helps children understand shame, is the week on *feelings*. Children are taught to identify their feelings, verbalize their feelings and look for options to deal with uncomfortable feelings. Some of the concepts used to teach children about their feelings are: all feelings are ok; it's important to have a vocabulary for all the feelings; it's important to identify difficult feelings; we have choices for our feelings; we cannot change other people's feelings.

Another week of group discusses the concept of *defenses* as well as that are built to protect each person. The following topic is addressed that intervenes with shame: children have a choice to keep their defenses exposed so as to cover up their true emotions or they can lower (not destroy) their defense when they feel safe and display what they are truly feeling and thinking so they can take on their part of the responsibility to become more intimate with others. This week gives children permission to expose shame at their own rate and keep them safe.

Another week of group focuses on *chemical dependency*. Most children feel at fault for the chemical dependency in their family, whether it is a parent or sibling who is addicted. Creatively teaching children that they are not responsible for the chemical dependency in their family is an important concept in shame intervention. Role playing situations can help children visually see they are not responsible for the drinking in their family.

Another week of group centers on the topic of *specialness*. The following topics can be addressed: strengthening the appreciation of each child's specialness, increasing the child's recognition of their special qualities and talents, building on the awareness of specialness of others, accepting the importance of friendships is important, celebrating each child as an important person. This topic intervenes with shame by reinforcing to the children that they are acceptable to another group of human beings. They can belong and be separate at the same time.

What builds trust in these groups is the structure and consistent facilitators who role model new behavior. Children are talked to individually and respected for their right to pass which helps them feel separate and in control. The adults in the group help nurture the children by modeling understanding, patience and acceptance of each person's feelings. Children are encouraged to verbalize feelings to the other children, recognition of positive qualities are highlighted and noticed and affirming messages are given to the children by facilitators. The educational process, the play, the structure, the affirmations and the group process continue to intervene with the shame of these youngsters by gently helping them recapture their childhood spirit.

CONCLUSION

Children may become developmentally delayed when they are raised in an alcoholic or chemically dependent family. The messages and behaviors that are needed for secure bonding and attachment are confused and inconsistent. Trust and security feelings become endangered when attention is focused on the alcoholic or on the alcohol. The isolation and abandonment that remains produces shame in these children. These children cannot complete the tasks in this beginning stage of development because they have not received the appropriate developmental affirmations. As children grow they need positive evaluation from family and peers – but they often become manipulative because they feel so worthless.

They feel incapable and do not feel as if they attained any mastery over their lives. They feel insignificant and unable to contribute to life. What they strongly need is a peer support group to assist with exchanging negative messages for positive ones. They need a place to re-establish trust with adults and a place to have play and laughter introduced with adult role models. The cycle of shame can be broken and the interpersonal bridge restored by the development of ongoing support groups for elementary age children of alcoholics.

A child's spirit can be rekindled when intervention of shame takes place.

REFERENCES

Ainsworth, M. & Bell, S., "Mother-Infant Interaction and The Development of Competence," in Connolly, K. & Bruner, J. (Eds.), *The Growth of Competence*, NY, Academic Press, 1974.

Belctsis, Susan C. & Brown, Stephanie, *A Developmental Framework for Understanding the Adult Children of Alcoholics*, Stanford University Medical Centers, Stanford, CA.

Briggs, Dorothy Corgill, *Your Childs Self-Esteem*, Dolphin Books, 1975.

Black, Claudia, *It Will Never Happen to Me*, M.A.C., Denver, CO, 1981.

Clarke, Jean Illsley, *Self-Esteem a Family Affair*, Winston Press, 1978, Minneapolis, MN.

Deutsch, Charles; DiCicco, Lena & Mills, Dixie J., "Services for Children of Alcoholic Parents, Casper Alcohol Education Program," Somerville, MA.

Erickson, E. H., *Childhood & Society*, NY: W.W. Norton, 1963.

Fossum, Merle & Mason, Marilyn J., *Facing Shame: Families in Recovery*, Family Therapy Institute, St. Paul, MN, 1985.

Fox, R., "The Effects of Alcoholism on Children," New York, National Council on Alcoholism Pamphlet, 1972.

Hawthorne, Terre & Sherman, Sue, "Celebrate You" Poem, 1979, Children Are People, Inc., unpublished poem.

Kaufman, Gershen, *Shame The Power of Caring*, Schenkman Publishing Co., Inc., MA, 1985.

Levin, Pamela, *Cycles of Power: A guidebook for the Seven Stages of Life*, 1980.

Lewis, Helen Block, "Role of Shame in Depression — Depression in Young People," *Developmental & Clinical Perspectives*, Guilford Press, Michael Rutter, Caroll E. Izand, Peter R. Rad, 1986, pp. 325-335.

Naiditch, Barbara & Lerner, Rokelle, *Children Are People Chemical Abuse Prevention Curriculum*, St. Paul, MN. 1983.

Naiditch, Barbara; Lerner, Rokelle & Hawthorne, Terri, *Children Are People Support Group Training Manual*, Children Are People, Inc., St. Paul, MN, 1985.

New Games Foundation, *More New Games*, Andrew Flugelman, (Ed.), Dolphin Books, Garden City, NY, 1976.

New Games Foundation, *The New Games Book*, Andrew Fluegelman, (Ed.), Dolphin Books, Garden City, NY, 1976.

Sexias, J., "Children from Alcoholic Families," In Estes, N.J. & Heinemann, M. Ed. (Eds.), *Alcoholism: Developmental, Consequences and Interventions*, St. Louis: C.V. Mosby, 1977.

Seixas, Judith S. & Youcha, Geraldine, *Children of Alcoholism, A Survivors Manual*, Crown Publishers, Inc., NY, 1985.

Stephanie, K. *Shamed Faced*, Haxeldon, 1986.

Sloboda, Sharon B., "The Children of Alcoholics: A Neglected Problem," *Hospital & Community Psychiatry*, Vol. 25, pp. 605, 606, 1974.

Videotaping in Groups for Children of Substance Abusers: A Strategy for Emotionally Disturbed, Acting Out Children

Don Efron, MSW
Kip Veenendaal, RegN, BSW

SUMMARY. This paper describes the use of a videotaping technique in groups of young children of substance abusers. The technique has been found to be particularly useful in working with very emotionally disturbed, acting out children. Use of video can be incorporated into the group at different stages in order to help children understand facts about alcoholism or other substance abuse, develop strategies for coping, and to help understand the roles which family members take in response to substance abuse. Vignettes of actual videotapes produced by children in the groups are presented. A strategic/systemic analysis of shame-based families is advanced to explain the efficacy of the videotaping method with deeply disturbed children. Considerations for the development of this technique are presented, including the question of involvement of parents.

INTRODUCTION

Young children of substance abusers often receive support and/or treatment in the form of peer groups (Hastings, 1984; Typpo, 1984; Hawley, 1981; DiCicco, 1983). There is ample evidence that such groups can be very useful for children of all

---

Don Efron and Kip Veenendaal are affiliated with the Madam Vanier's Children's Center in London, Ontario.

71

ages. Unfortunately, not all children are good candidates for inclusion in groups. In particular, deeply disturbed, acting out children are often excluded from such groups because of the disruptive effects they have upon group process.

In this paper, we describe our experience over the past two years of working with such children who have been included in our groups for children of substance abusers. We hope that our experiences, and the videotaping technique which we have developed to help maintain these children in the groups, will be useful to other individuals or group therapists in this field.

BACKGROUND

In the past two years we have led 7 groups of children of substance abusers at a Children's Mental Health Centre in London, Ontario. Altogether, 28 boys and 12 girls have attended the groups. The age range has been from 7-14 with the bulk of the children (29) between 9 and 11 years old. In all cases, there has been significant alcohol problems in the family. In 33 of the cases father or stepfather was specifically mentioned as the substance abuser. In 4 cases the mother was specifically mentioned. Grandparents, "boyfriends" and siblings of the child or child's parents were mentioned specifically as abusers in 8 cases. The substance abuser was still living in the child's home in less than 50% of the families.

Although a few of the children had suffered mildly from the substance abuse in the families, the typical referral describes a child whose family had been greatly disrupted by substance abuse. Most often the children had personally witnessed the deterioration of their parents' marriage because of the substance abuse. Angry confrontations, physical violence, accidents and even death of some family members had been part of their life experiences. Many had lost contact completely with the substance abuser though it was more typical for some contact, often sporadic, to have been maintained.

DESCRIPTION OF THE GROUPS

The theme of the groups has been both educational and thera-peutic. The 8 scheduled sessions have been designed to teach the children about alcohol, its effects on the alcoholic, ways to cope in living with or around an alcoholic, and the roles filled by members of an alcoholic's family.

The group produced positive results for most children. Many parents and child care workers reported improvement in the children's communications about the role of the alcoholic in their lives. Improvements were noted in their behaviors. In addition, many of the children genuinely enjoyed the group and looked forward to attending.

THE PROBLEM

This overall success did not blur two disturbing elements that reoccurred in group after group. First, the most "disturbed" children did not seem to benefit as much as others. Second, group control was extremely difficult to maintain despite the presence of two, sometimes three, group leaders in groups which rarely had more than seven children. Group "contagion" oc-curred rapidly and often escalated wildly. Typically, a session would go astray when the children were not "kept active." Dis-cussion times (such as after movies) and group work activities usually led to disastrous acting out. The acting out would be started by one of the "more disturbed" children and would quickly involve others. Eventually, the "good kids" would be drawn into the acting out or be submerged beneath the sea of noise and activity around them.

Two groups (#5 and #6 of the series), revealed the significant differences in our ability to work with the two types of children. In the 5th group, 3 of the 5 children were very active boys who had a long history of seeking, and obtaining, negative attention. The other group members were a mild mannered boy and a very quiet girl. From the beginning, group control was a major issue. Standard attempts to control group members by mild discipline, encouragement, or temporary removal from the group served only to exacerbate problems. Group leaders began to dread coming to the sessions while colleagues remarked on the extreme amount of noise and disruption from the group room. All attempts to have the children talk about their feelings in response to the materials presented failed miserably. The 6th group, by contrast, consisted of 6 children, only one of whom was identified as a negative attention seeker before coming into the group. Most of these children were also from a higher social economic status. Group control was easily maintained and there was no negative group contagion effect. Group leaders looked forward to group with only occasional comments about sporadic boredom. The extreme contrast between 5 and 6 only underlined what was apparent in all the other groups. Group leaders and group activities seemed to work well with children of substance abusers when those children were not significantly emotionally disturbed and negative attention seeking. Unfortunately, the neediest children seemed to be able to gain least from the group.

There was no question that the groups should continue—after all, most of the children were enjoying and learning from them. However, group leaders knew that unless some change occurred in the process and content of the sessions, those greatest at risk for emotional disturbances, alcoholism or drug abuse, and delinquency would benefit least from the group.

THE VIDEO TECHNIQUE

Group leaders had noticed one modality which seemed to contrast with the overall group pattern. Acting out decreased, and positive results increased, when the group produced a "video" about substance abuse and its effects. Repeatedly, the "stars" of the video—the ones who were the best actors and the ones who came up with the best ideas—were the same acting out, disturbed children who had been unable to participate effectively or positively in group exercises, discussions, art work, etc.

Group members were told at the beginning of the group that the group would produce a video. Originally, the actual videoing was begun in the 6th or 7th session. In later groups, we started videoing as early as the 2nd session. The children have been given the option of showing the film to their parents and have invariably accepted this option. Parents have been invited at the end of the 4th and 8th sessions to view the videos produced by the children.

We have found it useful to show the children films about alcoholism so that they have some basic sense of what a film about substance abuse would be like. The films often give them starting ideas or words which can be incorporated into the video. The group members are shown the video equipment and have the opportunity to see themselves "on t.v." before the actual videoing. The earliest videos deal entirely with alcohol or other substances and its immediate effects upon the abuser and family. The group leaders can use the films that have been shown as a base or can suggest that "other children" have done certain things in order to spark the ideas of the group. However, the main goal of the group leaders at this point is to elicit material from the group members to describe personal experiences which can be used in the video. Though the video focuses on alcohol and other substances in general, the children seem to feel safe enough to talk about drinking experiences they have seen both inside and outside their homes. It is usual for the more disturbed children to move from talking to displaying the behavior they have seen. They will stagger across the room, make bad jokes, talk loudly, etc.

At this point, the group leaders are able to introduce the idea of "making the video realistic" as the basic controlling device for the group. If, for example, a child begins to act so drunk or stoned that it becomes impossible to continue, the group leaders can always object to the behaviors on the basis that such behavior is not realistic. One of the group leaders, who has been a bouncer at a bar, can be called upon to give contrasting views of drunkenness. Children who are acting extremely loud can be asked to practice being a "quiet drunk." Thus the boisterous behavior can both be accepted as legitimate and at the same time controlled.

"Realism" also becomes a vehicle by which group leaders can constantly introduce new ideas to individual group members. Children who have been exposed to extreme violence can learn that this reality is but one of many. As with the "quiet drunk," the children can be exposed to the fact that not all alcoholics beat up their wives. The members who desire to have a "happy ending'' can be allowed one while at the same time ''realism'' can be used to suggest that an alternative ''unhappy ending'' might also be filmed. Similarly, if the children are exceptionally negative, an alternative positive ending could be suggested. Children who are too proud to admit that they might be scared in real life can be convinced to act ''as if'' they were scared for the sake of the video. A whole range of emotions can be dealt with in this manner.

Later videos deal with more advanced concepts. As the ''roles'' of the family members are presented to the group, the children can be asked to fill the roles for the sake of the video. It is possible to introduce the idea that they themselves often play roles in their lives and that they might alter the roles. The burden of the nonsubstance abusing spouse can be explored as well as the tendency of that spouse to ''take it out'' on the children. We have even found that it is possible to introduce the idea that the children ''might grow out of'' certain roles that have led them to be placed in the institution or to be considered as disturbed or delinquent.

EXAMPLES FROM THE VIDEOS

As indicated above, early videos tend to emphasize the fact of substance abuse and its immediate effects. Following is a brief edited sample of such a video:

Scene #1
Title: "Drunkbusters"

Theme: Hints to a child of an alcoholic.
Characters of Children: Dad, son, bartender, female patron, drunkbusters.
Scene in Bar: Bartender and female drinking.

Enter Father and Son
Female Patron: "Who is this little whipper?"
Father: "Son. Can I have a beer?"
Son: "Whiskey!!"
Father: "Give him a coke."
Female patron: "How you been?"
Father: "Good."

Female Patron: "How's the wife?"

Father: "Divorced."

Female Patron: (laughs) "I guess I haven't seen you in a long time. Pretty rough eh — Looks like a smart kid — Why did you and your wife get divorced?"

Father: "My drinking problem."

Female patron: "Who tells you it's a drinking problem — your ex-wife?"

Father passes out.

Bartender to Female Patron: "Want another drink?"

Enter Drunkbuster and places "NO DRINKING" sign on passed out father.

Female Patron: "Who are you?"

Drunkbuster: "I'm a drunkbuster!"

Drunkbuster turns to son.

Drunkbuster: "Your dad's been drinking."

Son: "I can see that — he fainted."

Drunkbuster: "Whenever your dad is drinking and he takes you with him, you should always have a spare quarter with you to use the telephone and a number — so you can call grandma for a ride home. That's about all — catch you later."

THE END

Later videos concentrate on family roles, as is shown by the following excerpt.

Scene #2
Title: "Home of Alcoholic Family"

Characters of Children: Father, mother, son (clown), daughter (hero).

Enter angry mother who has dragged drunken father from the bar.

Father: (shouting) "Why did you have to bring me back home?"

Mother: (angrily) "Because you're drinking too much!"

Father: "So who cares? I can drink as much as I want."

Mother: (angrily) "No you can't!"

Father: "Want a bet?"

Mother pushes father down.

Mother: "Sit down."

Clown Son: (excitedly) "Hi mom — hi — guess what I learned at school today?"

Clown Son: (continued) I learned this great joke — O.K. — Why did the chicken cross the road?"

Mother: (shouting and pointing) "Go to bed!"

Clown Son: "To get to the other side."

Mother: (shouting) "Go to bed!"

Enter heroic daughter.

Heroic Daughter: (Taking father by the hand) "Come on Daddy."

Father: (resisting) "I want to finish this argument with your mother."

Daughter pulls him down on the couch and covers him up as he passes out, daughter leaves the room.

Closing camera shot of mother looking angrily after the departed daughter.

THE END

SHAMELESSNESS, RESPECT AND THE VIDEO

Fossum and Mason suggest in their book *"Facing Shame"* (1986) that shame bound systems are ones in which violation of the person leads to shame, the self has vague personal boundaries, rules require perfectionism, and relationships are always in jeopardy. In contrast, in "respectful" systems violation of values leads to guilt, the self is separate but part of a larger system, rules require accountability and relationships are always in dialogue. They further suggest that once developed, shame lies dormant waiting to be activated. They present the idea that shame develops in a family system and perpetuates itself over generations as children develop poor sense of selves and poor boundaries. The family adheres to "rules" which emphasize control, perfection, blame, denial, unreliability, uncompleteness, not talking, and disqualification. The inherent tension residing in these families is typically expressed in an alternating tension — release cycle with "shame at the core."

Children from such backgrounds have a powerful tendency to

replicate such systems no matter where they are. Extremely disturbed shame-based children, especially those who have been placed in "scapegoat" or "mascot" roles, tend to use very overtly aggressive and visible means to accomplish such replication. It should be recognized that such replication is not in itself necessarily bad. By replicating, the children are exhibiting loyalty to their family and its rules while imposing a structure on a new system which allows them to function in a way that they can successfully compete with other children for positive rewards.

Though the rules are "shame-based," they are predictable and provide the only certainty and possible success for these children. They know how to handle such systems. In fact, as the videos suggest, they have a wealth of experience in surviving. In contrast, such children often feel coerced, unsuccessful and alienated in nonshamed-based systems.

This does not mean that the authors are suggesting that shame-based systems should be encouraged. Nor should children who come from shame-based families be restricted from nonshame-based systems. However, strategic/systemic thinking indicates that for change to occur therapists should modify a few elements of the system while deliberately maintaining others (Fisch, O'Hanlon, Watzlawick & Wilks). Changing a piece of the total system while allowing the rest to remain the same can allow the child to accept the change which can then be built upon to produce more changes. Given time this could lead to major shifts in personal functioning.

This analysis suggests that the most emotionally disturbed children of substance abusing families enter groups with an inbuilt and powerful ability to force the group into replicating a shame-based system. The hope of the group therapist must be to have tools available which will allow him the repertoire to meet this challenge. To do this the therapist must introduce respect into the shame-based system without directly challenging the system. It would seem that little is to be gained by challenging the child of a substance abuser to "be good." This merely replicates that system which leads to acting out.

Videotaping, as done in this group, is a technique which can be used to avoid the trap of either allowing the shame-based system to be replicated or alienating the child. Videotaping can make use of the child's scapegoating and distracting tendencies for this purpose. We have observed that many of the deeply disturbed children strive to be in the limelight. Presumably, such "shamelessness" develops because of the need in the family to avoid focusing on the painful realities of substance abuse. The clownish, delinquent behaviors might also develop as an attempt by the child to force attention to be paid to him in order to have basic needs met. No matter what the "cause" of the shameless behavior, it seems certain that its continued existence prevents peers and adults from establishing a respect-based system with the child. Attempts to be respectful are met with acting out, which in turn, is usually followed by attempts to control the child through rewards or punishment. This quickly establishes a conflictual situation in which even if the adult wins the battle of controlling the child he loses the war. Thus, in the group, as in most other areas of the child's life, the child's shameless behaviors serve to force the entire system toward the coercing, blaming, and shaming model with which the child is all too familiar.

Videotaping is different in that the feeling of shamelessness need not be eliminated in order for the video to succeed. In fact, the shamelessness is an attribute which can easily be used to enhance the video. In this context, the child's "shamelessness" does not mean that he has to act out negatively. Rather, he can be "fearless" in front of the cameras. In this way, the acting out child can get the success and recognition normally available to him only in shame-based systems. At the same time, his ideas and feelings which he might otherwise hide from prying negatively perceived adults can be portrayed and accepted. Control and new ideas can be introduced by the group leaders as being necessary for "realism." This validates the child's expressions while at the same time allowing him to "save face" by not having to be confronted head on with contrasting values and ideas. Finally, the rule of secrecy can be both expressed and controlled through the videotaping. Children can express what has been happening in their families while at the same time being assured that the parents will see it in a disguised form. Thus, the content is both presented and hidden in a way which is familiar, comfortable and safe to them.

In our last group, one ten year old boy's experience suggests the power of the video technique. "Jim" comes from a very disturbed family with a long history of alcoholism and violence. He himself witnessed physical abuse and was subjected to it. Jim had an extremely difficult time in the group. He was extremely active, with learning disabilities, and an inability to utilize discussion or art. Physically, he presented as extremely shamed (Potter-Efron). When other children would act out, he would quickly fall into line with them and the group would remain precariously balanced between control and chaos. Jim was not liked by other group members nor did he act in any way that he could be liked. Though he desperately needed attention and acted out to get it, he knew of no positive ways to give attention to others. In general, he acted far more immature than his age. Jim's initial reaction to the possibility of videotaping was negative. Two other acting out boys in the group reacted positively to the video but Jim appeared to be so ashamed that he could not bear to see himself on t.v. nor to show the video to his mother. Jim's acting out escalated to the point where it seemed that he might disrupt the videotaping for the entire group. For example, when asked to portray the role of a son in the group during an early video he said he would not do it and even attempted to hide under the couch. Fortunately, the video was about reactions to alcohol. It was suggested to the group member portraying the "father" that he would come in drunk and be angry at his son no matter what Jim did. Thus, Jim's acting out negative attention seeking behavior was found to be both acceptable and indeed useful for the purposes of the video. The video then proceeded and Jim, true to his words, at first refused to cooperate. As his "father" began to get angry at him, Jim began to do a little acting. Jim was both eager and frightened to see the results of the video. In later videos, Jim was able to participate and even, at the end, to contribute ideas for the videos.

Jim was perhaps the most shamed child that we have worked with. "Roger," the "clown" in "scene 2," was more typical. Roger was a 12 year old boy attending our Day School facilities. Roger had repeatedly been kicked out of schools for negative behaviors. In the group he presented as egotistical and boasting. He would not admit to feelings of fearfulness or weakness of any kind. Though possessing many nice qualities, Roger was not particularly liked by group leaders or group members because of his great need for controlling others and because of his bragging. Roger responded well to the idea of the videos and though he attempted to control them his behavior was far more acceptable in this setting than when other activities were introduced. As the group talked about the roles of the children, particularly the "distracter," they were able to pinpoint Roger as being the "clown." Roger's forced joke telling was very clear in the videos. It was suggested by the group leaders that the "mother" would be mad at him for distracting even though he was trying to prevent conflict from occurring. Roger himself suggested that if this happened his response would be one of sadness. He then vividly portrayed a hurt and crushed child leaving the scene after his mother had chastised him while he made a joke to try to cheer up father. Thus, Roger had moved from being completely unable to admit any feelings of sadness to being able to show them in this video.

DIRECTIONS AND CONCERNS

At this point, we are still developing the videotaping technique. We are concerned that on occasion videotaping can slip into replicating shame-based systems. Most of the time using this technique we have been able to accept without confrontation the shame-based systems. However, on occasion, group leaders have unintentionally replicated the shame-based system in the group. For example, if the group leaders become too concerned with "producing" the video they can start to take a position of rejecting the child. As the children are extremely sensitive to such rejection, the value of the videoing can be lost. The videoing seems to ensure that the group leaders will have a fighting chance to avoid replicating the original shame-based system. However, they must be constantly on their toes, flexible and tolerant to avoid negative interactions. It is far easier for them to be successful in this than with other modalities but nevertheless, the technique does not insure success.

Another concern is with parents viewing the videos. Originally, we had parents view the videos produced by children while in the room with them. We found though that there was a tendency for the parents of the more disturbed children to react negatively to the video. We now believe that it was asking too much of the parents to "enjoy" the videos. It would seem likely that watching the videos produces a feeling of shame within the parents. One parent in particular made comments that the video seemed to be portraying the family as being disturbed. Some of the parents got angry at the children while watching the videos and would yell at them or otherwise attempt to control them.

In review, it seems likely that the group leaders had fallen into the trap of trying to force the families out of the shamed-based systems by inviting the parents to come in and view the videos with their children in front of the therapist. The parents felt shamed and reacted with hostility, which of course was directed toward the children rather than to the therapist. We have now developed an alternative model. A therapist who has not been involved with the children in the group meets with the parents, shows them the videos, and requests that they serve as "consultants" to the group leaders. The therapist in charge of this meeting takes a neutral role in regard to the video, neither praising nor condemning it (Imber-Black, 1986). This approach promises to be much more productive. Parents have responded favorably to it. They have been able to verbalize their anger toward the drinking partner. More importantly, they have been able to tell the therapist that they are concerned that the children are not seeing the pain which they themselves went through. In one group, the mothers suggested that the children do a video on the problem of the nondrinking spouse. This information was then relayed back to the children. We are currently considering ways in which this bridging between the two groups can result in positive growth for both children and their parents.

CONCLUSION

Deeply disturbed, acting out children of substance abusers can benefit by being in a group for children of substance abusers. However, common techniques which work with other children have a tendency to fail when utilized with this client group. In contrast, having the children produce video tapes on the theme of substance abuse and the effect it has upon those living with substance abusers allows the therapist and group members to gain control of the situation. We have speculated that positive results are obtained because the video allows therapists to accept the need of the children to express shame-based system rules while in group. The use of video allows expression of "shameless-ness" by the children without producing negative conflicts between children and group leaders. Respect for the children can be introduced in this manner without direct confrontations and challenges to the shame-based system. The techniques allow therapists to have a much greater chance of interacting successfully with emotionally disturbed acting out children of substance abusers. The technique also lends itself to involvement of the non-drinking parents in such a way that dialogue can begin between them and their children.

We believe the videotaping technique can be developed in the future to be a meaningful tool for the therapist interested in helping deeply disturbed children in a group work setting. Videotaping can help the children explore what has happened to them, how it is currently affecting their lives, and even the potential danger for them in the future if they cannot change the roles ascribed to them as part of growing up in a substance abusing family.

BIBLIOGRAPHY

Black, Claudia, *My Dad Loves Me, My Dad Has a Disease,* Denver, Colorado: MAC, 1979.

Cork, Margaret, *The Forgotten Children*, Don Mills, Ontario: General Publishing Company, 1969.

DiCicco, Lena et al., "Recruiting children from alcoholic families into a peer education program," *Alcohol Health and Research World*, Winter 83/84: 28-34.

Fisch, R., Weakland, J. & Segal, L., *The Tactics of Change*, San Francisco: Jossey-Bass, 1983.

Fossum, Merle A. & Jason, Marilyn J. *Facing Shame*, New York: W.W. Norton and Company, 1986.

Hawley. Nancy P. & Brown, Elizabeth L., "The use of group treatment with children of alcoholics," *Social Casework*, 1981, 62 (1): 40-46.

Hastings, J. & Typpo, M., *An Elephant in the Living Room*, Minneapolis: Compcare Publications, 1984.

Imber-Black, Evan., Workshop Presentation, London, Ontario, 1986.

O'Hanlon, Bill, "Splitting and linking: Two generic patterns in Ericksonian therapy," *Journal of Strategic and Systemic Therapies*, 1982, 1, 21-25.

O'Hanlon, Bill, "Strategic pattern intervention," *Journal of Strategic and Systemic Therapies,*" 1982, 1, 26-33.

Potter-Efron, Ronald, "Shame and guilt: Definitions, processes and treatment issues with alcohol or drug abusing clients," *Alcoholism Treatment Quarterly*, 1987, (364).

Typpo, M. & Hastings, J. *An Elephant in the Living Room: A Leader's Guide for Helping Children of Alcoholics*, Minneapolis: Compcare Publications, 1984.

Watzlawick, P., Weakland, J. & Fisch, R. *Change*, New York: W.W. Norton, 1974.

Wilks, James, "Context and know how: A model for Ericksonian psychotherapy, "*Journal of Strategic and Systemic Therapies*, 1982, 1, 2-25.

From Guilt Through Shame to AA: A Self-Reconciliation Process

Ed Ramsey, MEd, CAODAC

SUMMARY. This article differentiates guilt and shame as aspects of each individual. It also discusses the relationship between shame, guilt, and alcoholism and chemical dependency. The Twelve Step Program of AA is identified as a resource for resolving guilt, shame, and alcoholism. The concept of AA as a caring community is discussed on the basis of how AA addresses issues related to shame and guilt.

Shame and guilt are aspects of each person that sometimes overlap but can be differentiated. Both are deeply related to the development and perpetuation of alcoholism. In order to differentiate shame and guilt, one needs to define the concepts.

SHAME

Shame is an experience affecting the whole self. It affects all the person's life powers: physical, emotional, mental, spiritual, volitional, and social. It is a judgment of the self, leaves the person feeling visible, vulnerable, defective, worthless, powerless, isolated, and alone. Consequently shame tends to be more subjective and internal in its focus than guilt.

Ed Ramsey is in private practice with First Things First in Eau Claire, WI.

GUILT

Guilt tends to be associated with behavior. It is related to inappropriate moral behavior which produces a belief that "what I did was bad." The primary focus for guilt tends to be more external and consequently more cognitive and objective.

ALCOHOLISM, SHAME, AND GUILT

Alcoholism has been called a disease of feelings. An alcoholic can be defined as a person whose drinking causes problems in any area of his life and in spite of said problems continues to drink (Ramsey p. 55). Another definition of an alcoholic is that an alcoholic is a person whose drinking costs him more than money as a person pays for his drinking at the expense of self-esteem and self-worth. His drinking has become harmful and the person has become enmeshed in guilt and shame. Vern Johnson (1972) observes "it appears that alcoholism does not exist without the presence of guilt. A basic description of chemically dependent people is that they are guilt-ridden people" (Johnson p. 77).

Alcoholism results in a pattern of dysfunctional behavior which leaves the alcoholic person feeling guilty. This guilt can get transferred into shame in several ways.

The alcoholic person believes that he should be able to control and change the consequences of his drug-related behavior. But when he is unable to change or control that behavior, he perceives this inability to change as a failure and a falling short. The person will continually try to change and fail, which in turn creates an attitude of "I must be a failure." This attitude inflates the person's sense of powerlessness, and as the person's sense of powerlessness and failure increases due to his inability to control his behavior, the person begins to change his attitude from "what I did was bad" to "what I did was wrong, and I must be a bad and weak person for doing it." This new attitude represents a bridge from guilt to shame.

Another bridge to shame results from society's attitude toward the alcoholic. There is a myth in our culture which implies that alcoholics choose to be the way they are. This assumption leads to a judgment of alcoholics as being weak and bad and deserving of punishment. Thus we have a condition which is called a disease but is treated as a crime. Alcoholics are judged and punished for experiencing behavioral manifestations and symptoms of their disease (Ramsey p. 69).

This is a cultural contradiction which judges the person and his behavior as bad. This external judgment tends to reinforce and validate the attitude of the alcoholic "that I am weak and bad and others feel the same way about me." Thus, the alcoholic is judged as both guilty and shameful by society.

PUNISHMENT

Our culture punishes alcoholics for acting as such. This external punishment serves to validate guilt and shame and for the guilt-ridden person, it absolves the guilt by punishing the behavior.

The shame-based person feels the need to punish his whole self because of his attitude that "what I did was bad, and I am a bad person for doing it." The need to punish one's self is at the heart of shame-based behavior. Shame-based compulsive behaviors are designed to punish and abuse the self for being a bad person. Shame-based people may abuse alcohol as a form of self-abuse. It is when alcohol becomes self-abuse that the person has progressed from feeling guilty into feeling shameful.

CHARACTEROLOGICAL CONFLICT: FROM GUILT TO SHAME

Shame, guilt, and alcoholism are characterological issues. Characterological conflict is a prerequisite for these conditions.

In order to understand this phenomenon, it is necessary to define characterological conflict. For the purposes of this paper, characterological conflict is defined as the emotional conflict that results when a person's behavior is inconsistent and/or in conflict with his values. This conflict between a person's values and a person's behavior serves to split the self. This split of the self is the basis for shame-based behavior. Kaufman (1980) describes the function of shame-based identity as "a process by which the self within the person begins to actively disown parts of the self thereby creating splits within the self.'' Any act of transgression which is viewed as bad or wrong produces characterological conflict. Vernon Johnson (1978) suggests that alcoholism can only exist where there is a conflict between the person's values and the person's behavior.

The person who experiences characterological conflict will initially experience guilt, because the focus is on the behavior which the person perceives as bad or wrong. When the badness is validated externally by others, the person becomes ashamed of being a guilty person. Miller (1983) calls this phenomenon "moral shame." It is at this point that the disassociation (split) of the self begins, because at this point the person changes his focus from "what I did was bad" to "I am a bad person for doing this." The key to this transition is that the wrong doing is now perceived as involuntary, thus producing shame both in relationship to the behavior and also in the loss of self-control. The loss of self-control combined with the perception of total badness and/or defectiveness of the self serves to eliminate the concept of choice, thus making the behavior involuntary and shameful. The sense of being out of control produces a feeling of vulnerability, powerlessness and of being seen. With this sense of vulnerability comes the need to defend the self.

DEFENSE STRATEGIES: PARALLELS BETWEEN SHAME AND ALCOHOLISM

Defensive strategies against shame parallel the defensive against alcoholism.

Withdrawal

Withdrawal is the most commonly used defense against shame and alcoholism. Withdrawal is a desire to hide and/or avoid. People who withdraw have been called runners from life (Potter-Efron). For many shamed persons, addictive substances and behavior provide a means of running and/or withdrawing from the fear of facing themselves. Forms of withdrawal include the classic alcoholism symptoms of denial, rationalizing, minimizing, distracting, and avoidance.

Grandiosity

Grandiosity is often a defense against shame and alcoholism and is possibly the opposite or other extreme from withdrawal in that the person attempts to deny his perceived defectiveness, inadequacy, vulnerability, and shame by trying to appear superior. The person may speak or boast about his faults or problems. The person will engage in pretentious, flashy behavior in an attempt to draw attention to his or her defectiveness. This may be an attempt on the part of the person to survive internal conflict caused by his shame/alcoholism. The person's survival involves identifying with the shaming behavior in a way that makes others believe that this is the way the person chooses to be. In order to do this, the person must deny his real values and self in favor of shame producing values and inappropriate behavior. This situation serves to intensify the characterological conflict and leads to additional shame and inappropriate behavior. In relationship to shame, this particular defense is manifested in the form of condescending behavior. By putting himself above another, he denies his own defectiveness and vulnerability. This serves only to reinforce alienation and isolation from others which can additionally contribute to the shame process.

Grandiose behavior serves to delude its victim more than any other and as a defense against alcoholism it is so common that Jellinek identified it as part of the symptomatology of the disease (Ramsey). When grandiosity fails to protect the individual from his vulnerability and shame, the person will likely intensify the defense. Grandiosity intensified is frequently expressed by another defense against shame and alcoholism, perfectionism.

Perfectionism

Perfectionism, like grandiosity, is a defense designed to compensate for one's perceived failures and defectiveness. It is an attempt to deny one's humanness, inadequacies, and frailties by trying to appear better than everyone else. The alcoholic tries to avoid looking at himself, thus perpetuating his shame and inappropriate behavior. It serves only to delay inevitable feelings of inadequacy and incompetence that grow at the center of self-respect. The frustration inherent in trying to be perfect can lead to a sense of failure and self-resentment that gets manifested through rage.

Rage

Rage as a defense against shame and alcoholism results from an attitude of "the best defense is a good offense." Kaufman suggests that "rage manifests itself in either hostility toward others or bitterness. Although this hostility and bitterness arises as a defense to protect oneself against further experiences of shame, it becomes disconnected from its original source and becomes a generalized reaction towards almost anyone" (Kaufman, p. 86).

Rage as a defense against alcoholism is manifested in a disease symptomatology as unreasonable resentment and aggressive behavior to compensate for loss of self-esteem and self-worth. The defense of rage represents a survival reaction when other defenses fail to protect the self. The person is saying in effect "I cannot survive exposure of myself and I will attack you if you come any closer" (Potter-Efron).

Rage is initially projected onto others, but because of the shame inherent in losing control and abusing personal power, the rage is inevitably and eventually internalized and directed toward the self. When rage is projected onto the self, there is perceived need to punish the self for "being bad." This self-punishment which is subconsciously motivated is expressed in the form of shame-based behaviors such as the compulsive addictive behaviors mentioned previously.

Compulsive Addictive Behaviors

When shame manifests itself in the form of compulsive addictive behaviors, the behavior itself becomes a defense against the shame. Alcoholism and chemical dependency insulate the person from shame by altering the person's mood.

Addiction also allows one to avoid confronting the shamed self. The addiction provides the escape through a preoccupation with addictive behavior. The intensity of the addiction is in direct proportion to the shame and the person's fear of confronting the shamed self.

Defenses against shame and alcoholism are avoidance strategies that enable the problem to progress and worsen. However, the alcoholic may eventually reach a point where he has to abandon his defenses and face the reality of his need for help in order to cope with his problems.

THE ALCOHOLICS ANONYMOUS COMMUNITY: A SAFE AND CARING ENVIRONMENT

In order for the shame-based person/alcoholic to abandon his defenses and face reality, he must be exposed to a safe and caring environment where he can begin to face the split self, his vulnerability, and his dysfunctional behavior. The safe, caring environment affords an opportunity for the person to begin to accept his defective self and thus begin the reconciliation process: shame begins to heal when exposed in a safe environment.

The AA community can provide a safe and caring environment in which the shamed/addictive person can begin to heal. The very nature of AA is such that a person's sense of vulnerability is decreased. The preamble of AA defines this basic principle (AA World Services, p. 564):

> Alcoholics Anonymous is a fellowship of men and women who share their experience, strength and hope with each other that they may solve their common problem and help others to recover from alcoholism. The only requirement for membership is a desire to stop drinking . . . our primary purpose is to stay sober, to help others achieve sobriety.

Alcoholics Anonymous avoids judgments, labelling, and shaming the person by requiring the person to be only himself. This principle is reinforced by eight of the twelve AA traditions.

Tradition 1

"Our common welfare should come first; personal recovery depends upon AA unity" (AA World Services, p. 561). This tradition reinforces the value of caring and the need to be concerned about others when sharing one's own experience. This behavior helps the alcoholic resolve guilt issues related to past behaviors that have harmed others. It also helps him face the vulnerability issues related to his shame by letting him reach out to other people in a caring way which contributes to developing a sense of oneness.

Tradition 3

"The only requirement for membership is the desire to stop drinking" (AA World Services, p. 564). This tradition avoids the validation of shame inherent in labeling the person with the stigma of alcoholism.

Anonymity is the cornerstone of AA. This is evidenced by the fact that six of the twelve traditions emphasize, support and reinforce anonymity.

Tradition 4

This is the first of the anonymity traditions. "Each group should be autonomous except in matters affecting other groups or AA as a whole" (AA World Services, p. 564). This tradition helps to reduce vulnerability and reinforces a sense of safety by helping ensure privacy and minimizing exposure for the alcoholic shame-based person.

Tradition 6

"An AA group ought never endorse, finance or lend the AA name to any related facility or outside enterprise, lest problems of money, prestige or property divert us from our primary purpose" (AA World Service, p. 564). This tradition ensures safety by reinforcing privacy and minimizing public exposure.

Tradition 7

"Every AA group ought to be fully self-supporting, declining outside contributions" (AA World Services, p. 564). This tradition reinforces anonymity and safety by guaranteeing privacy and freedom from outside financial obligations.

Tradition 10

"Alcoholics Anonymous has no opinion on outside issues; hence the AA name ought never be drawn into public controversy" (AA World Services, p. 564). This tradition reinforces safety by minimizing exposure, controversy, and conflict.

Tradition 11

"Our public relations policy is based on attraction rather than promotion; we need always maintain personal anonymity at the level of press, radio and films. Our relations with the general public can be characterized by personal anonymity . . ." (AA World Services, p. 564). This tradition also reinforces the safety of the AA group by minimizing exposure and reinforcing privacy and anonymity.

Tradition 12

"And finally we of Alcoholics Anonymous believe that the principle of anonymity has an immense spiritual significance. It reminds us that we are to place principles before personality; that we are actually to practice a genuine humility. This is to the end that our great blessings may never spoil us; that we should live forever in thankful contemplation of Him who presides over us all" (AA World Services, p. 564). This tradition reinforces the value of anonymity as a very personal experience and the value of each individual's own personal identity as validated by a Higher Power.

The guarantee of anonymity is important for alcoholic/shamed persons because it protects against exposure and helps to guarantee a safe environment where the individual can begin to face his shame and inappropriate behavior and to deal with it.

The shamed/alcoholic individual will initially use the AA group as a safe environment to begin to face shame, but as the person works the program and the steps and as the reconciliation process evolves, the person must begin to face his shame outside the AA group. AA calls this "carrying the message." If the individual is unable to face his shame outside the group he can never fully reconcile it and may become dependent upon the AA group. This step is reinforced by Tradition 5.

Tradition 5

"Each group has but one primary purpose — to carry this message to the alcoholic who is still suffering" (AA World Services, p. 564). This tradition reinforces the value of reaching out and sharing one's own vulnerability with others in a way that facilitates self-acceptance and self-reconciliation.

THE BIG BOOK

Chapter Five in *Alcoholics Anonymous* (1955) (often called the Big Book or the Bible of AA) describes how the program works. It is titled simply "How it Works." This chapter includes many terms which suggest that to resolve shame issues and alcoholic behavior in a way that will endure one must address the issue completely. The absoluteness of recovery is contingent upon the person being willing to go to any lengths for his recovery. The chapter indicates that complete honesty with oneself is necessary for recovery. It goes on to describe the process of honesty as a sharing of the shamed self through stories of "what we used to be like, what happened, and what we are like now." This sharing of the shamed self is essential to recovery and to reconciliation of the self for it is the admitting and accepting of one's vulnerability and shameful behavior that one begins to resolve it.

The turning point occurs when the alcoholic/shamed person hits bottom. This bottom is described by Moustakas in his book *Loneliness* (1961): "The fundamental communion in which we suffered enabled him to get to the very depths of his experience. Perhaps in arriving at the foundation of his grief and loneliness, immediate death or immediate life were the only choices within reach. He chose to live. From his rock bottom loneliness emerged a new life and the real self was restored" (Moustakas, p. 73).

Hitting bottom is a prerequisite for reconciliation and resolution of the problem. This allows the reconciliation process to begin because it is at this point that the person can explore himself and out of desperation begin to recognize that he is powerless to resolve these issues on his own. At this point the person can begin to recover through the twelve step program of AA.

THE TWELVE STEPS OF AA

The twelve steps of AA are an outline for the reconciliation of the self. The following is a discussion of each of the twelve steps (see Table 1) with a description of how they address shame and guilt issues in the alcoholic/shamed person. It is important to realize at this point that there are no experts on AA and recovery. The following is simply an interpretation of the steps and include insights and ideas that I have found useful to me both in my own personal recovery and in working with alcoholic/shamed persons.

Here are the steps we took and *suggested* as a program of recovery.

Step I

"We admitted that we were powerless over alcohol — that our lives had become unmanageable" (AA World Services, p. 59).

The first step is probably the most important and one of the most difficult steps to take. It addresses both shame and guilt and taking this step is a prerequisite for recovery and self-reconciliation. Unless this step is taken the rest of the twelve steps are unnecessary.

Shame Components

The fear of powerlessness is a seedbed for shame because for many people to feel powerless is to be defective, inadequate, and to fall short of what one expects from oneself. The fear of powerlessness facilitates a sense of vulnerability and defectiveness. Powerlessness for many people implies helplessness because of the attitude that "I must be in control and if not something is wrong with me." It is this vulnerability and feeling helpless that produces shame.

Table I. SHAME AND GUILT ISSUES ADDRESSED BY THE 12 STEPS

STEP	SHAME	GUILT
1	Powerlessness	Unmanageability
2	Internalization of powerlessness	Restoration to sanity (wholeness)
3	Making a decision to take the power back through the surrender process	
4	Making an inventory of the self	Focusing on behavior in taking the inventory
5	Exposure of faults	Exact nature of wrongs through behavioral experiences
6	Surrender process	Unloading the bad behavior
7	Humility	Shortcomings with its behavioral focus
8		Reconciling inappropriate behavior
9		Reparations for inappropriate behavior
10	Inventory process	Admitting wrong behavior
11	Self validation by a Higher Power	Acceptance of fallible human behavior
12	Validation of new restored whole self, Sense of belonging	Self validation through new, changed behavior

The need for power is a basic need and when one is deprived of a basic need one feels insecure, inadequate, deprived, vulnerable, and shamed. At this point many people confuse being powerless with being helpless and being helpless with being worthless. It is important to help people realize that their power exists in what they can do about the problem, not in trying to control it. Kaufman (1983) calls this "taking the power back."

Defenses against the fear of powerlessness are the same as the defenses against shame. Alcohol and other drugs can be used as a defense against powerlessness because alcohol and drugs can give a person a sense of power and control. In order for the person to face one's powerlessness without the drug one must also face the shame inherent in the alcohol and drug problem.

Guilt Components

"That our lives had become unmanageable" is the last part of the first step that focuses upon the consequences of one's inappropriate behavior. This focus on behavior or the idea that "what I did was bad" produces guilt. There is also a sense of shame related to the perceived abuse of power and personal control. The shame that is related to being out of control and powerless can be a bridge from guilt because the wrongdoing is experienced as involuntary. The person can go from feeling that the behavior was bad and that they abused their personal power to an attitude of "I am bad and worthless." The person in essence becomes ashamed of being guilty (Miller, p. 47). This sense of moral shame can lead to one of the biggest barriers to recovery and self-reconciliation — blame.

Shame, Guilt and Blame in Step 1

Blame is a barrier to recovery and self-reconciliation in that blame becomes the bridge between guilt and shame and becomes internalized in the form of self-blame. Self-blame is the opposite of self-acceptance and powerlessness. A person who blames himself is in effect denying his powerlessness and is saying he had a choice over his behavior and "I am bad for behaving in the way that I did." This self-judgment implies culpability and leaves the person feeling more shame and guilt.

Consequently, blame is not only an obstacle to recovery and reconciliation; it actually intensifies the problem and contributes to it.

The internalization of shame and self-blame is a destructive process which results in the need to punish oneself. Self-punishment, which is a reflection of internalized shame, manifests itself in the form of self-neglect, self-sabotage, and self-abuse. The following is a discussion of these three behavioral manifestations.

Self-Neglect, Self-Sabotage, and Self-Abuse

Self-neglect occurs when because of stress, low energy level, and negative attitudes toward the self, the person begins to ignore himself physically, emotionally and socially. This neglect can lead to serious physical and emotional problems. The person who blames himself for his situation is also likely to engage in self-sabotaging behavior in an attempt to restore the emotional balance between a positive reality and his perceived low self-worth and self-esteem. This self-sabotage represents a form of internalized blame and self-abuse. A person will harm himself through sabotaging something that is important to him (job, school, relationships, health, and/or finances).

Self-abuse is the result of a person who perceives himself as bad and feels a need to be punished. Alcohol, drugs, food, gambling, compulsive sex and sexually abusive behavior, and physical neglects or physically abusive behaviors all represent forms of self-abuse. Also, self-neglect, self-sabotage, and self-abuse all contribute to make a person's life more unmanageable, reinforcing and increasing shame and guilt. If this cycle is not reversed, it can lead to chronic disease and premature death.

Step 2

"Came to believe that a power greater than ourselves could restore us to sanity" (AA World Services, p. 54).

This step is a continuation and internalization of Step 1, because it is only when one internalizes the concept of powerlessness that one will perceive the need for help. This need for a sense of power from outside the self can be shaming for some people because for them to need help from others or from outside the self is totally unacceptable. The second step makes the need for help acceptable by allowing a person to believe that getting help is appropriate and necessary if the person is to recover.

Shame component. The internalization of powerlessness helps the individual who experiences shame in relationship to having needs, accept the idea that he needs help from outside himself. The internalization of powerlessness involves accepting and facing one's limitations, defectiveness, and vulnerability. In order to do this, one must begin to face and reconcile his shame.

Guilt component. "To be restored to sanity" implies a restoration of health and wholeness. This restoration involves reconciling one's inappropriate dysfunctional behavior with oneself. Only by accepting the effects of one's alcoholism, including guilt-producing irrational behavior and thought, can the person begin to restore his ability to think clearly and act morally.

Step 3

"Made a decision to turn our will and our lives over to the care of God as we understand him" (AA World Services, p. 59).

The third step deals primarily with the resolution of shame. The concept of making a decision implies that one has choices. According to Kaufman, the idea of having a choice over things that affect one is the experience of power: "to experience choice is to know power" (Kaufman, p. ix). This step reinforces the sense of power by requiring the person to focus his attention on his will and his life, not his problems, thus helping him that the power is not over the problem but what he does about it. This power is not over the disease but in recovery.

This step also differentiates AA as a spiritual rather than a religious program by leaving the definition of a Higher Power up to the individual. The person can define his Higher Power in a way that is significant to him, whereas a religious approach defines this Power for the individual. This is important for the person who feels shamed because he has violated his religious beliefs. Many alcoholics believe that they are bad, sinful and defective and will "burn in Hell." The idea of "God as we understood him" allows the person to define God as a God of caring, love, and forgiveness rather than a God of wrath.

The first three steps of the twelve step program lay the foundation for the reconciliation process by breaking the shame/blame cycle and by helping the person accept his powerlessness and take back some of the power. These steps are primarily externally oriented, helping to resolve guilt and the shame being a guilty person by relieving culpability. Reconciliation of the self is, however, an internal process and Step 4 changes the focus from external to internal. This step initiates the person's survey of the damage to self.

Step 4

"Made a searching and fearless moral inventory of ourselves" (AA World Services, p. 59).

Shame component. Making a moral inventory of the self is the point where the person starts to survey the damage to the shamed self. Facing the shame of self is necessary if one is to accept the shamed self and begin to reconcile the defective self.

Guilt component. The guilt component involves focusing on the behavior necessary to identify the damage to the self. AA calls this behavior "character defects." If one sees character defects as primarily behavioral then this step would deal primarily with guilt. However, character defects can also imply internalized guilt and shame and if seen in this way, this step deals primarily with shame. As with Step 1, alcoholic guilt and shame are entwined and consequently this step addresses both issues and can be used to focus upon either.

Step 5

"Admitted to God, to ourselves, and to another human being the exact nature of our wrongs" (AA World Services, p. 59). Step 5 is the validation and continuation of step 4.

Shame component. The admission of one's defects to oneself, to God, and to another human being results in the exposure of one's faults. To face the risk of exposing one's faults to another and to own one's sense of falling short is the essence of being honest with oneself. Honesty is essential to the reconciliation process because it is dishonesty and defensiveness that facilitate a sense of vulnerability and fear of exposure which contribute to the feeling of shame. Consequently to risk exposure and to share one's vulnerability is to begin to reconcile the shameful behavior with the self. Being honest with others by defining one's wrongs helps the person to reconcile a sense of shame with oneself. By making the shame public and by owning it in front of others, it makes that shame more acceptable to himself. Sharing these feelings with others allows the person to accept his shame in a non-threatening way, especially if others are accepting of the person in spite of the behavior.

Guilt components. The term "exact nature of our wrong" implies specific behaviors or experiences. Confessing these behaviors helps the person to resolve them. This confession prepares the way for the alcoholic to make amends for his behavior later in the program.

Steps 6 and 7

"We're entirely ready to have God remove all these defects of character" and "Humbly asked him to remove our shortcomings" (AA World Services, p. 59).

Shame component. The act of turning one's shame over to a Higher Power serves to help absolve a person from the responsibility for it and sets the stage for self-acceptance through humility. There are situations when a person's shame and blame are so overwhelming that the person cannot resolve them alone. The sixth step suggests that a person allow a power greater than himself help to resolve these wrongs. This process reinforces the acceptance of powerlessness while providing a means by which a person can take some of the power back (that is through utilizing a Higher Power for help).

Guilt component. These steps help the individual resolve his sense of guilt by turning inappropriate dysfunctional behavior over to a power greater than himself. When he surrenders his guilt to a Higher Power the individual admits that he cannot control that behavior entirely on his own. He needs and is now ready to accept the help of his Higher Power and the AA community. Steps 5, 6 and 7 initiate the resolution of guilt. Steps 8 and 9 validate this process.

Steps 8 and 9

"Made a list of all persons we had harmed and became willing to make amends to them all" and "Made direct amends to such people whenever possible except when to do so would injure them or others" (AA World Services, p. 59).

Up to this point the individual has reconciled himself internally, but to validate the process and to reinforce it, there is a need to begin to clean up the effects of a life made unmanageable by alcoholism. This step deals primarily with guilt because at this point the person begins to assess the damage to his life and to others as a result of his inappropriate moral behavior. This making up also helps validate the reconciliation process by providing the individual with opportunities to behave in a way that is more consistent with his true values. This congruence is essential to the reconciliation of the self because it was the incongruence between values and behaviors that initiated the disassociation of self.

Shame, like alcoholism, is never totally resolved. No matter how together and healthy the person becomes there is always the potential for relapse and/or having the shame validated. Consequently, the last three steps of the 12 Step Program are the maintenance steps designed to support, reinforce, and maintain recovery over a long period of time.

Step 10

"Continued to take personal inventory and when we were wrong promptly admitted it" (AA World Services, p. 59).

Step 10 deals with both shame and guilt. It is very important because it is a continuation of Steps 4 and 5, and it perpetuates the self-inventory and honesty process.

This process is essential to self-reconciliation and recovery. This step means that the person must continue to inventory the defective self and to be honest about his defectiveness in order to accept it and to prevent it from revalidating shame and reinitiating disassociation of the self.

Shame component. This step, like Steps 4 and 5, helps resolve shame by requiring the person to face his shame, accept it, and then risk exposure by being honest with others about his defectiveness.

Guilt component. "That when we were wrong promptly admitted it" implies that one must be honest about his behavior. It is this focus on one's inappropriate behavior that helps resolve guilt. By acknowledging his misbehavior the recovering alcoholic can renew his commitment to living a sober and responsible life.

Step 11

"Sought through prayer and meditation to improve our conscious contact with God as we understood him, praying only for knowledge of his will for us and the power to carry that out" (AA World Services, p. 59).

This step helps the individual maintain a trusting relationship with a Higher Power, thus continuing the absolution process and helping give the person a sense of value and worth as validated by a Higher Power. This step also reinforces the value of being human and showing humility in that it suggests that a person be more concerned about what his Higher Power wants from him rather than what he wants from his Higher Power. This attitude tends to suggest that it is appropriate to allow a Higher Power to be in charge.

Shame component. Seeing God as a God of love and striving to improve our conscious contact with this entity helps a person to begin to develop a sense of value, worth and wholeness through validation by his Higher Power. The concept of seeking knowledge of His will for us rather than our will for Him reinforces this idea of humility and can help facilitate the acceptance of oneself as a fallible human being.

Guilt component. Accepting one's human behavior as fallible and perceiving one's behavior as God's will for us helps to alleviate the sense of immorality that accompanies alcoholic behavior. It relieves the individual of the entire responsibility for his disease but still gives him hope for a better, moral life. The recovering alcoholic's new behavior will be more consistent with his basic moral character when he is able to share responsibility with his Higher Power.

Step 12

"Having had a spiritual awakening as a result of these steps, we tried to carry the message to alcoholics, and practice these principles in all our affairs" (AA World Services, p. 59). Step 12 is the final step and the end result of the Twelve Step Program and deals with both shame and guilt.

Shame component. Step 12 does not indicate that the end result of the 12 Step Program is abstinence or sobriety, because neither one of these words is in the steps. It describes the result of these steps as a "spiritual awakening." This spiritual awakening results from the realization that "I am valuable and worthwhile as a human being and I do not deserve to be punished." This new awareness and acceptance of self is a byproduct of the reconciled self. The reconciled self absolves shame because the person can only reconcile the disassociated self through self-acceptance, self-caring and elimination of his sense of badness, defectiveness and shame. Once the self is reconciled, one can then reach out to carry the message to others in a caring, supportive way. Through owning his alcoholism the person turns a situation that had been a liability into a resource or an asset. Rather than isolating the person from others his alcoholism actively brings him closer to people, thus facilitating a sense of belonging and caring.

"To practice these principles in all our affairs" is to validate one's recovery and reconcile the self through behavior that is consistent with one's values. This validation of the new valued self serves to perpetuate recovery. In the past one's behavior was a reflection and validation of one's problems and shame. Once the self is reconciled the new behavior of the recovering alcoholic needs to validate and reflect his sense of value, worth and self-caring.

CONCLUSION

Guilt, shame and alcoholism are characterological issues that overlap but can be differentiated. Shame is a judgment that the self is bad. Guilt is a judgment of behavior as bad. The alcoholic initially experiences emotional pain in the form of guilt related to his inappropriate behavior but translates this guilt into shame.

A sense of shame in turn produces a feeling of vulnerability and defectiveness. This serves to initiate a disassociation (split) of the self. This disassociation of self results in more shame. The defenses of withdrawal, grandiosity, perfectionism, and rage appear to protect the self. When these defenses fail the individual recognizes his need to be helped.

The Twelve Step Program of AA is an outline for the reconciliation of the self in recovery. Each step addresses specific issues related to shame and guilt. The AA community offers a safe and caring environment for a person to risk exposure of his shame in order to resolve it. The traditions of AA reinforce this safety through anonymity. The person can make amends with his shamed self and reconcile his dysfunctional behavior through utilization of the Twelve Steps.

Once the shamed self has been reconciled and accepted, the new positive self must be validated and supported behaviorally through the practice of a way of life that reinforces this new self.

Finally, it is important to remember that this article is suggested as an interpretation of the AA Twelve Step Program and is to be used only as a guide. As such, it is suggested that you take what you can use and leave the rest.

REFERENCES

Alcoholics Anonymous, AA World Services, NY, 1955.

Johnson, Vernon, *I'll Quit Tomorrow*, NY: Harper and Row, 1972.

Johnson, Vernon, "Intervention: The Technique of Presenting Reality in a Receivable Way," Rutgers Summer School of Alcohol Study, 6/28/78, Rutgers University, New Brunswick, NJ.

Kaufman, Gershen, *Shame: The Power of Caring*, Cambridge, MA: Schenkman, 1980.

Kaufman, Gershen, *The Dynamics of Power: Building a Competent Self*, Cambridge, MA: Schenkman, 1983.

Miller, Susan, *The Shame Experience*, Analytic Press, 1985.

Moustakas, Clark, *Loneliness*, New York: Prentiss Hall, 1961.

Potter-Efron, Ronald, "Shame and Guilt: Definitions, Processes, and Treatment Issues with AODA Clients," *Alcoholism Treatment Quarterly*, Vol. 4(2), Summer, 1987.

Ramsey, Ed, *Handbook for the Chemical Abuser and Those Concerned*, Eau Claire, WI: Bartingale Press, 1984.

Substance Abuse, Shame and Professional Boundaries and Ethics: Disentangling the Issues

Lindsay A. Nielsen, CCDP, SW

SUMMARY. The author addresses the special professional boundary concerns and ethics faced by therapists in their work with chemically dependent individuals and their families. Substance abusers and recovering chemically dependent counselors are identified as two populations especially vulnerable to boundary inadequacy. Included is a continuum which illustrates professional boundary issues/boundary violations, and recommendations for both the prevention and intervention of boundary violating behavior.

INTRODUCTION

The discussion of professional boundaries and ethics is crucial when exploring the process of shame for recovering chemically dependent people. There are a number of relevant issues to consider. The experience of guilt and shame is an inherent consequence of boundary violation, regardless of the nature of the relationship or the severity of the violation (Nielsen, 1984, 6-10; Coleman & Colgan, 1986). When the violator is someone in an authoritative role, the intensity of the shame for the victim often increases, as the victim is more likely to blame her/himself. It has been recognized that the process of substance abuse significantly alters boundary functioning, and that boundary inadequacy is widely found in chemically dependent families (Coleman & Colgan, 1986). The presence of boundary inadequacy

---

Lindsay A. Nielsen is in private practice in Minneapolis, MN.

109

leads to boundary violation, which is seen clinically in the higher rates of both childhood physical and/or sexual abuse, and current family violence patterns in the chemically dependent population (Nielsen, 1984, 6-10; Evans & Schaefer, 1987).

These issues are especially relevant for counselors as the therapeutic relationship greatly influences the restructuring of boundaries or the reinforcement of existing relational patterns. Professional boundary dilemmas are a normal part of the therapeutic relationship, but it is imperative that these be resolved appropriately for the client's well-being, and for the well-being of the counselor and the organization. The process of professional boundary maintenance becomes more difficult if a counselor has problematic personal boundaries. Many recovering chemically dependent people, and recovering or nonrecovering adult children of alcoholics become counselors. These counselors may show significant personal boundary inadequacy which can lead to professional boundary violations.

Boundary issues are a necessary part of any counseling relationship. Some are easily handled but some are exceptionally complex. Questions of ethical concern are raised daily, often with conflicting answers. No counselor is able to therapeutically sort through all the issues in isolation.

It is also the hope of the author to challenge the notion that only "bad" counselors violate the boundaries of the clients, and "good" or competent counselors are not vulnerable. Counselors and therapists violate client boundaries for a myriad of reasons. "Neediness," loneliness, personal crisis, lack of self-care, ignorance, and a history of victimization are all cited as reasons therapists exploit clients to meet their needs (Coleman & Schafer, 1986, 341-344; Schoener, 1984). Only a small percentage of offending therapists can be described as sociopathic or mentally ill. When we narrow the issues to good vs. evil, we miss the real issues which are relational. In most cases of boundary violations, clients experience great emotional turmoil due to conflicting feelings about the offender. In a shame-based philosophical framework (Good/Bad), we also lose the understanding and preventive possibilities offered by the use of a continuum.

Professional boundary dilemmas confront us daily, for they are part of a complex system of interacting. If we were to ascribe to the notion of "keep it simple" in this case, we would be forcing ourselves back into the language of shame: good/bad, wrong/right, and easy/hard. We need to allow ourselves continuums, and the language of complexity.

DEFINING PROFESSIONAL BOUNDARIES

Professional boundary maintenance is the process of setting and maintaining boundaries specific to one's professional role, taking into consideration all that accompanies that role. In counseling we need to assess our role, our client's vulnerabilities and the nature of our particular therapeutic setting.

Consider the dynamics of a counseling relationship which differentiates these boundaries from other types of relationships:

1. Clients enter the counseling relationship trusting us to act on their behalf at all times, simply by virtue of our role as counselor. This means that they assume we will make decisions that are in their best interest regardless of our personal situation, and regardless of whether we are "on duty" or "off duty,"
2. The client enters the counseling relationship from a position of need.
3. The client assumes the counselor is the expert, so will know better what is best for the client.
4. Every counseling relationship involves the process of transference and counter-transference.
5. All of these components interact to create a disparity of power. The counselor always has more power than the client. Due to this disparity of power the client never has true power of consent with the counselor. For example, even if the client initiated a romantic relationship, or if the client agreed to a sexual relationship with her/his counselor, this isn't considered true consent.

Professional boundaries are built atop personal boundary structures. These professional boundaries are learned in a number of arenas. Professional boundaries and ethics are to date minimally taught in academic settings. Boundaries are also taught and modelled in clinical settings both from peers and supervisors. Law and ethical codes describe some ethical guidelines as does agency policy and formal and informal job descriptions.

Unfortunately for many clinicians, good training on professional boundaries and boundary violations has been all but absent from most of their training, academically and clinically.

Professional boundaries are also learned through experience. This learning tends to be more powerful than other types of learning. If a counselor (as a client) experiences serious boundary violations from another counselor, or a teacher, or a parent or other authority figure, then s/he is being taught both a behavioral system of boundary intrusions, and is also being taught the belief system which rationalizes the behaviors. If a counselor experiences appropriate boundary maintenance, this experience will also be translated into training for the role of counselor.

Every counselor has "blind spots," some of which change with life circumstance. If a life situation closely parallels a client's, there is a greater risk of boundary problems at that time. Boundary issues are clearly an integral part of the therapeutic process. In order for the counseling to be effective there must be trust, transference, care and concern. Boundaries play an integral role in all complex interactions, and boundary dilemmas and vulnerabilities will always be present. This author is in no way prescribing that the therapeutic relationship become a rigid, non-humanistic interaction of traditional psychoanalytic flavor. Resolving the boundary issues positively, in order to provide a healing experience, is crucial. Modelling healthy relational boundaries teaches skills in restructuring boundaries in other relationships as necessary. Given the generational nature of boundary inadequacy, this is imperative for our clients and their families.

Professional Boundary Violations

Defining professional boundary violations is more difficult than defining professional boundaries. A violation is different from a boundary issue. Boundary issues are a necessary part of the therapeutic relationship. Professional boundary violations are those boundary issues that when not appropriately addressed, become harmful to the client, or refer to those boundaries which should never be crossed by a counselor.

It is helpful to conceptualize therapeutic boundary issues and violations on a continuum. The existing literature clearly shows that severe professional abuses, such as a counselor having sex with a client, is often the final stage in a series of less severe violations (Coleman & Schaefer, 1986, 341-344; Nielsen, Peterson, Shapiro & Thompson, 1986). Boundary problems can be defined as all of the beliefs and behaviors exhibited by the counselor that in some way move the client from client status while s/he maintains client vulnerability.

As has been shown with familial incest (Evans & Schaefer, 1987; Nielsen, 1984, 6-10) the underlying belief system and preceding emotional and psychological violations are often just as harmful as the "overt" behaviors. This concept also applies to professional boundary violations. Consider the following continuum for professional violations.

<————————————|————————————|————————————>

Underinvolvement	Therapeutic Range	Overinvolvement
Neglect-Boundaries do not allow for appropriate connection.	Boundary issues are resolved therapeutically. The boundaries allow for appropriate connection and separation.	Counselor is too involved with the client. Too much connection.

Counselors can exhibit boundary problems that fall into the category of neglect or underinvolvement. Failure to return phone calls, indiscriminately cancelling sessions, nor paying due attention to the therapeutic needs of clients, failing to acknowledge the emotional connection between themselves and their clients, failing to say goodbye appropriately, etc., are all examples of neglectful boundaries or underinvolvement. Clients who are neglected will experience all of the consequences of boundary violations, just as from those of overinvolvement. neglect is inherently shaming. Clients question what they did wrong, and why they're not important enough to warrant attention.

The therapeutic range includes boundary issues and dilemmas.

The counselor is appropriately involved with the client. There is a therapeutic balance between separation and connection. The generational boundaries are clear. The counselor doesn't abdicate his/her role, and the needs of the client are appropriately weighted and addressed.

In the overinvolved range there is too much connection. The needs of the client are not appropriately focused on. The counselor may attend only to the client's needs for connection without therapeutically balancing with the client's needs for separation. The counselor abdicates her/his role as s/he moves the client out of client status. Some examples of severe violations include: accepting expensive gifts from a client, borrowing money from a client, physically assaulting a client, or being sexual or romantic with a client. All of these situations fall on one extreme end of the continuum of boundary violations. While few counselors would argue that these are boundary violations, they still occur with frightening frequency.

Between 10-17% of the counselors researched admitted having sex with one or more clients (Kardener, Fuller & Mensh, 1973, 1077-1081; Brudsky, 1986). This statistic is probably conservative and doesn't include severe violations of a nonsexual nature. Fifty percent of the psychiatrists surveyed by Grunebaum, Nadelson, and Macht, stated that they knew of cases where a therapist was being sexual with one or more clients or patients. Few had reported the situation. These statistics don't include situations involving "former" clients or patients. The research to date also fails to address emotional boundary violations.

As was stated earlier, boundary dilemmas can be resolved in a healing and therapeutic manner or can be acted on inappropriately, and cause great harm to a client. The following model was developed by Nielsen, Peterson, Shapiro, and Thompson for the Minnesota Task Force on Sexual Exploitation by Counselors and Therapists Manual, 1986. Included here is a condensed version of the model. The model is intended to illustrate situations of boundary issues and boundary violations in the therapeutic relationship. The levels, when placed on a continuum show the progressive nature of boundary violations. As such, the end of one level is the beginning of the next. The consequences to the client do not necessarily gain in severity congruent with the continuum.

```
I<————————————————————————————————————————————>I
Level One      Level Two      Level Three      Level Four      Level Five
```

Level One

> BOUNDARY ISSUES ARE UTILIZED TO IM-
> PROVE THE THERAPEUTIC RELATIONSHIP
> AND TO HELP THE CLIENT MEET THEIR
> GOALS THROUGH POSITIVE RESOLUTION.

At this level counselors feel confused and uneasy about some aspect of the therapeutic relationship. S/he finds her/himself questioning, evaluating, and second-guessing himself. Something is not right but the counselor is not certain what it is. Some examples of these kinds of boundary issues include:

— A client asking his or her counselor extremely personal questions and the counselor responding by giving the requested information rather than by setting appropriate therapeutic boundaries or by exploring the meaning of the question to the client.
— A client repeatedly phoning the counselor at home during the night and the counselor failing to set limits.
— A client being verbally abusive to the counselor when angry and the counselor failing to set limits.

These boundary issues are in the therapeutic range, and are not considered violations. Not resolving them, however, can be the beginning of more serious problems. When addressed appropriately, boundary issues in this level teach the client through positive boundary restructuring. These issues are a normal part of the therapeutic process.

Level Two

> BOUNDARY ISSUES IN EFFECT IMMOBILIZE
> THE COUNSELOR, WHO IS THUS UNABLE TO
> UTILIZE THEM TOWARD THERAPEUTIC GAIN
> WITHOUT OUTSIDE CONSULTATION.

As in Level One, the counselor feels uneasy and confused, but now also begins to attend to the client in a "special" way. The self-evaluative process has moved to one of obsessing. The process of second-guessing has progressed to the point where the counselor's ability to trust him/herself impaired. In the later stages of this level the counselor begins to lose sight of the client's therapeutic goals. Examples of Level Two boundary issues include a counselor:

— Feeling "stuck."
— Failing to attend to a client's boundary crossings.
— Attending to the client in a "special" way.

Level Three

> BOUNDARY VIOLATIONS INCLUDE BEHAV-
> IOR ON THE PART OF THE COUNSELOR THAT
> IS THERAPEUTICALLY HARMFUL TO THE CLI-
> ENT.

The feelings of uneasiness have now progressed to a growing sense of anxiety. Feelings of guilt and shame blanket much of the therapeutic relationship. The counselor is feeling even more stuck as s/he now feels an even greater need for secrecy. The role-confusion intensifies and the counselor begins to feel helpless and victimized by the client. Examples of Level Three violations include a counselor:

— Viewing a client as a peer, or failing to see the client as a less powerful or vulnerable person in the relationship.
— Making decisions based on his/her needs rather than based on the needs of the client, such as:
   — Self-disclosure for nontherapeutic purposes.

—Inviting and encouraging the client to support the
counselor.
—Breaking organizational rules like meeting a client
away from the agency.
—"Protecting" the client from other counselors.

Level Four

BOUNDARY VIOLATIONS OCCUR IN WHICH THE COUNSELOR OVERTLY EXPLOITS THE CLIENT.

The counselor by this time has rationalized, denied and minimized the exploitive behavior. S/he may no longer be conscious
of feeling any guilt or shame. A great deal of energy is invested
by the counselor in self-protection. The client is also engaged in
the process of protecting the counselor. Examples of Level Four
violations include:

—Sexual contact with client(s).
—Engaging the client to protect the counselor.
—Making financial deals with clients, going into business to-
gether, etc.

Level Five

THE COUNSELOR RATIONALIZES THE EXPLOITIVE BEHAVIOR AND ORGANIZES HIS OR HER LIFE AROUND A DELUSIONAL SYSTEM.

Counselors in this stage display a massive distortion of reality.
They have organized their life around the delusion that the exploitive behavior is acceptable and even helpful to the client.
This exploitive behavior may be of an emotional, sexual, or financial nature. An example of Level Five functioning includes
the chemical dependency counselor who believes that the rules
and ethics should be changed to permit sexual contact between a
counselor and a client when "it is in the client's best interest."

Characteristics of Boundary Violations

One major effect of boundary violations is the experience of shame as one of the primary consequences. It is common for victims to ruthlessly question themselves as to their behavior, their motives, and their response, or lack of response, rather than hold the violator accountable. "What did I do wrong to make this happen?" or "How did I handle this badly?" are questions often asked by victims.

The process of boundary violation involves the loss of something important and valued, a loss that the person often has no control over. Rationally, a betrayal of trust is experienced. Further loss occurs for the victims, because they distance from others in their lives due to the secrets connected to the violation.

Consider the following case example:

> Sally has been seeing her counselor on and off for about three years. The counselor was her primary counselor in chemical dependency treatment and saw her individually during aftercare. After not seeing the counselor for some time, Sally returned to do periodic therapeutic consultations with him. Although the relationship had seemed to change and become less formal, Sally still "looked up to him," and felt like she depended on his support. During their last meeting, the counselor told Sally that he felt he had fallen in love with her, and would leave it up to her as to how to proceed.

In this situation, Sally experiences great emotional turmoil. While she has done nothing wrong, regardless of what she decides, she will lose the relationship as it is. This constitutes a very real death. She will never be the same, and the relationship, past and present, has been significantly altered. Her memories and understanding of the relationship takes on a new meaning. Sally feels angry, betrayed and protective. She feels the need to keep the situation secret so people won't judge the counselor whom she cares for or think she did something bad to make this happen. Sally experiences distance in her other relationships. She feels unable to openly discuss the situation with her AA group, as the counselor is known in the community. She also feels afraid to consult another counselor.

Consequences of Boundary Violations

There are direct and indirect consequences of boundary violations. It appears that the severity of the violation doesn't impact the inclusion of specific responses. Boundaries which are violated in a "small" way will include the same components as when boundaries are violated in a "larger" or more severe way. The response is to the process of violation as well as the content.

The direct consequences are those immediately involved with the violation. The indirect consequences are those which grow out of the process of violation, or are connected with the direct consequences but in some way become chronic. An example of this can be seen with abuse victims. The direct consequences include, but are not limited to, any physical injuries and immediate feelings that are experienced. The indirect consequences include the more chronic fear of intimacy and vulnerability, having a high tolerance for abusive behavior, shame, irrational guilt, grief and loss, anger and rage, learning to take responsibility for the behavior of others, loss of trust in yourself and others, and disassociation.

People attempt to cope with feelings associated with violation in many ways. We know that one way is to self-medicate. Chemical use is an effective, though destructive way to alter the feelings associated with boundary violations. When a person stops ingesting the mood-altering chemicals there is often a resurfacing of the feelings, with or without conscious memories.

Another way of attempting to cope with boundary violations is to avoid those people or situations in which there has been a violation. This is difficult if the violation occurred in the context of a trusting and close relationship. As avoidance in this case is usually impossible, people find other ways to cope that often increase their stress and produce harmful consequences.

Examples of How Clients Invade or Violate a Counselor's Boundaries

Clients clearly bring their boundary problems with them into treatment or therapy. In effect it is their job as clients to exhibit the boundary issues therapeutically that they experience in other relationships. It is, however, always the counselor's job to redraw the therapeutic boundaries, regardless of the client's behavior. Some examples of client boundary crossings and violations include:

- Asking the counselor extensive personal questions.
- Trying to pursue a friendship or peer relationship with the counselor.
- Entering the counselor's office without knocking.
- Telling abusive, sexist or racist jokes.
- Verbal or physical abuse of any kind.
- Spatial violations (standing too close).
- Sexualizing the therapeutic relationship.

These boundary problems and violations can be directed at the counselor or at other clients or family members. When giving a client feedback about boundary concerns it is most effective to be specific, including examples. It is also effective to redraw the boundaries when feasible. This enables the client to learn experientially. Redrawing the boundaries will also trigger shame, so it is therapeutically helpful for the counselor to be firm, kind and emotionally present with the client.

While these examples are specific and concrete, boundaries are reflected in so many ways that the relationship between client and counselor needs to be in focus.

SPECIAL CHARACTERISTICS OF THE SUBSTANCE ABUSING POPULATION

We are working with an especially vulnerable population in terms of shame and boundary inadequacy. The very process of substance abuse alters and confuses boundaries and reinforces shame. This confusion in combination with altered values leaves treatment-seeking substance abusers developmentally vulnerable. This condition of vulnerability is part of the reason that treatment is successful. During this period people are especially open to learning a new value system. This confusion, however, also renders them less able to clearly question anything that does not feel right, like therapeutic boundary problems. Their guilt and shame tells them that anything bad that occurs is their fault.

Many ACAs are exceedingly loyal so once past their initial, oftentimes rigid set of boundaries, will stand by a counselor or group member regardless of the cost to themselves. As so many ACAs have been neglected, they are especially vulnerable to those who show care for them. They in effect are searching for "good" moms and dads. It is easy for counselors to become "gurus" which is not in the best interest of the client.

Characteristics of Chemically Dependent Families in Relation to Boundary Inadequacy

It is helpful for counselors to know their own family of origin boundary patterns so as to have greater insight regarding specific professional boundary vulnerabilities.

In some families the process of individuation or boundary formation is hampered by the parents' inability to "let go" of their children either physically or emotionally. This type of family would be called "enmeshed." In an enmeshed system the boundaries within the family are too diffuse. Members tend to over-involved with each other and not involved enough with others outside the family system. In an enmeshed system, children are shamed for having individual needs. They are told in different ways that they are "bad" if they have separate or conflicting feelings or ideas from other family members.

A client from an enmeshed family system will exhibit the belief system and accompanying behaviors in the treatment process, and will attempt to both merge with the counselor as well as fight the counselor's attempts at setting boundaries that allow for appropriate connection and for appropriate separation. The client is likely to react with shame and rage.

In other families the process of individuation is interrupted by the parents' inability to be connected to their children in the first place. This type of family would be called disengaged or under-connected. In a disengaged family the boundaries within the family are too rigid. While in an enmeshed family a child's autonomy needs are being neglected and shamed, in a disengaged family the child's dependency needs are neglected and shamed.

Children from disengaged families feel unimportant and will come and go in relationships as if they don't impact upon anyone else. The treatment process will trigger shame as it teaches connecting and emotional responsibility. As clients they will bring with them their lack of trust in relationships and their belief that no one has the right to expect anything from them or from relationships in general. They also believe it is unacceptable to ask for anything from anyone directly. They literally need to be taught that appropriate boundaries with peers allow for some interdependence, and that appropriate boundaries with counselors allow them to be appropriately dependent.

SHAME-BASED FAMILY SYSTEMS

We also know that one of the characteristics of chemically dependent family systems is that they are often shame-based. Problems (when they are addressed) are addressed by assigning blame. Instead of identifying the problems and looking for possible solutions, the family identifies a culprit. The system becomes so depleted due to the addiction that there is too little nurturing and attention to go around. The processes of denial and rationalization render the adults in the family unable to be honest about the system's depletion. In this case the children are often shamed simply for having needs and feelings. This occurs both through the process of neglect and through active shaming.

Children's needs are not met, so they feel "bad" for having them. They are also told that their needs or feelings are bad or wrong. The children may be labeled as "crazy," selfish or spoiled simply for being children. If the children openly express their feelings they are shamed as a method of control. If the feelings were openly acknowledged the adults would have to acknowledge the realities of the addiction and other problems, which they are not ready to do. Children are often taught to mistrust their feelings and perceptions. This mistrust translates into boundary inadequacy and a heightened sense of shame.

The belief system that accompanies behaviors can be just as problematic in treatment for clients and for counselors. Consider the power of these beliefs:

— It is bad to make mistakes; mistakes prove that I am not "good."
— If you get close enough to me you will find that I am not "O.K."
— There is good and there is bad, with nothing in between.
— If I am good and we disagree, then you must be bad (or vice-versa).
— If you are good you won't make mistakes, because mistakes are proof that you are bad. So if you make mistakes then you must be bad, and I am also bad for having misjudged you.

All of these beliefs impact the process of boundary maintenance. Unless addressed as a family systems loyalty issue, clients are unable to modify their boundaries as necessary.

It has been estimated that between 25 and 80% of substance abusing clients seeking treatment have been physically or sexually abused. These statistics are frightening in terms of the frequency of abuse in these families. They are also indicative of the high rate of boundary dysfunction that we see in our client population.

Other characteristics of chemically dependent families relevant to this topic area include crisis orientation, authority issues, external locus of control and communication dysfunction. All of these issues involve shame and specific boundary problems.

Crisis Orientation

In a crisis-oriented system you either lose or never learn the skills initially which are needed to accurately assess situations. This limits a person's ability to prevent crisis as well as hampers the ability to respond appropriately to crisis when it can't be avoided. In a crisis-oriented system so much energy is directed at "putting out fires" that there is little energy left for noncrises. Children learn that in order to get their needs met they must have a crisis. Members also learn to bolster their self-esteem by dealing with crises. Clients with these issues will attempt to "seduce" the counselor into paying undue attention to their crises.

This process translates in treatment as a client constantly pushing a counselor's boundaries. A crisis needs immediate attention regardless of time or place. If someone feels shameful or unworthy s/he will not be able to trust that someone will care for, and pay attention to her/him simply because "you're you." By pushing boundaries, clients try to take control to "make" the counselor attend. If this process is uninterrupted clients miss the opportunity to discover what would happen if they don't manipulate the outcome. They also fail to trust that the care that is offered is genuine. It is imperative for a counselor to address this issue, and to set firm limits, even though it will trigger the shame of the client. A client in this situation will probably have an intense emotional response. In fact the response may even become another crisis. While this is uncomfortable for everyone involved the process can be a positive one.

Simply telling a client that crisis orientation can be harmful does little to truly interrupt the process. Holding firm on one's boundaries models the issues as well as helps the old feelings surface. Clients can then learn to trust that they will be attended to outside of a crisis, even when they don't "force" or manipulate others.

A counselor who has unresolved crisis orientation issues will also create crises to get their attention, recognition, and nurturing needs met. They may do this at the expense of their clients or their program. They will be unable to set limits with clients and they are at greater risk for professional burn out. Crisis orientation is a drain on the energy reserves of everyone.

Authority Issues

In dysfunctional families children are often raised by adults who have difficulty handling their power appropriately. The children may become accustomed to both role reversal and a blurring of the generational boundaries. The children learn to compensate for incompetent authority. When power is abused, children are placed in a position of trying to avoid further abuse. One way to do this is to "take care" of the person in power. Trying to reduce the authority figure's stress level by taking over responsibilities, becoming invisible, entertaining, and not requiring supervision or assistance are all ways that children in this situation attempt to gain protection.

In these situations children are not given consistent and appropriate limits, which results in a general lack of safety and developmentally appropriate learning. Children grow up not understanding how to use these rules or how to appropriately challenge those with whom they disagree. Children then assume a defiant or compliant stance toward authority. The belief is that either one completely and literally follows the rules or one must battle and "bleed" and completely defy the rules. No middle ground is recognized.

As adults, they try to neutralize the power held by authority figures because incompetence is automatically assumed. One method of neutralization is to act like peers with, or to reverse roles with those in authority. Counselors are authority figures, and fall into the category of assumed incompetence.

It is crucial for counselors to hold the line, kindly and competently. If we enable clients by allowing them to neutralize our authority, we are neglecting their needs. It is essential for the healing process that clients experience competent authority. Otherwise a client will be unable to distinguish family of origin dysfunction from healthy boundaries.

Communication Problems

Communication patterns in chemically dependent family systems tend to be indirect, nonassertive, and shaming (Nielsen, 1984, 6-10). One of the consequences is that the children learn to pay more attention to covert (hidden) messages than overt (open) ones. This process requires the merging of boundaries. Paying excessive attention to others is one way to protect yourself from an emotionally or physically painful attack. This overattention to other person's feelings, needs, and problems is at the very core of codependency.

Clients with this external locus of control may totally define themselves based on their perceptions of other's expectations. Counselors, and group members are closely watched for signs of disapproval, anger, pleasure, fear, and shame. Misperceptions frequently occur. When reality testing doesn't take place, the misperceptions are incorporated into the belief system about how "I should be." Clients then change their behavior to be loved and approved of. Quite often they make incorrect translations, and make changes which negatively impact their relationships. They may also go against their own values which becomes part of their shame. This process results in the loss of their true selves as well as the demise of their relationships.

Children of shame-based parents will learn creative but exhausting ways to caretake their parent's shame so as to avoid seeing their parent's self-hate or feeling the rageful attacks. It is frightening for a child to know the level of self-hate their parent(s) experience. They know that they are part of their parents, and their parents a part of them, so they feel hated as well. This process of caretaking is often continued in subsequent relationships with the desperation level of a child fearing abandonment or attack.

Counselors with unresolved communication problems will assume that they can accurately "read" a client or colleague without reality testing. Counselors with serious communication problems are also unable to model appropriate and clear communication for clients.

COUNSELOR CHARACTERISTICS

When studying professional boundaries and the impact on clients, it is useful to look at the characteristics, not only of the client population but also of the counselor population.

In the discussion of family characteristics, specific types of issues were identified. Obviously, unresolved family of origin issues can lead a counselor to cross client boundaries inadvertently. There is certainly the possibility present to overidentify, or in some cases, underidentify with the client. The question then becomes one of, "Where do I really stop and where does the client really begin?" In these situations, it is tempting to prescribe for the client (especially where family matters are concerned from a base of personal decisions or history rather than from a clinical or theoretical framework). Counselors may over or underestimate client's abilities, by seeing them as being "the same as me."

The effect on the client in terms of shame is complex. On one hand, knowing that someone they highly respect has gone through similar struggles may serve to reduce their shame. It can also be liberating to see someone talk with pride and acceptance about that which they feel so shameful. On the other hand, it may increase their shame to see the counselor handling with apparent ease that with which they themselves are struggling so desperately.

Counselor's Self-Care Patterns and Professional Codependency

How a counselor manages self-care issues will impact the boundaries they exhibit with colleagues and clients.

Counselors are more likely to set appropriate boundaries with clients when their nurturing, intellectual and support needs are met through other relationships. Counselors that are feeling lonely, neglected, bored, or unappreciated are more apt to use clients to fill these personal and professional voids.

Issues of self-care are continuous. At different times counselors will have different vulnerabilities. During any period of personal or professional crisis a counselor will be more vulnerable to boundary problems.

The field of counseling offers endless opportunities to behave codependently. The very nature of this article clearly outlines the needs of the client as primary. Some counselors justify not taking care of themselves as a way of putting the client's needs first. However, if counselors fail to take care of themselves, they will be unable to ethically attend to their clients. The idea of helping and being paid for it is a rewarding notion for many nonrecovering codependents who feel little choice in the process of caretaking.

Significant boundaries are crossed through the process of professional codependency, both with clients and colleagues. Codependency involves specific, disrespectful behaviors and a belief system that support them. Attending to others' feelings, needs, and problems at the expense of your own well-being is one of the primary characteristics. Behaviors of concern include:

- Making decisions to withhold important information due to concern about a client's or colleague's reaction. The concern is more for the comfort level of the counselor than for the well-being of the client or colleague.
- Seeking approval in a way that interferes with one's professional functioning.
- "Crisis functioning."
- Compulsion to fix everything or "overfunctioning."
- Taking too much responsibility for the outcome of the therapy or treatment.
- Losing sight of "whose work is whose."
- Enabling colleague's and client's inappropriate behaviors.
- Not taking care of yourself, due to over-attention to others.

Counselors need to be careful of anything they feel they shouldn't talk about with a particular client. Often it's the client's no-talk rules in which we have become entangled. Counselors can enable clients through a process of relieving their shame for them, or by trying to avoid it altogether.

The process of profession codependency hurts both the client and the counselor. The client has contracted the professional services of the counselor. This contact is made with the implicit understanding that the counselor will behave professionally and ethically. A counselor who fails to set appropriate limits which ensures both the counselors and clients well-being in an ethical manner is clearly failing to hold to his or her contract.

The engagement in codependent behaviors with each other as a staff puts counselors, their clients, and their organization in serious jeopardy. Simply acknowledging that one is codependent is not enough; recovery is mandatory in order to maintain appropriate therapeutic boundaries.

SIGNS OF SHAME
IN THE THERAPEUTIC RELATIONSHIP

It is essential for the counselor to be able to identify shame when it is present in the therapeutic relationship. It is the counselor's job to be able to set limits when a client's shame is intruding on the boundaries of other clients, or on the counselor's boundaries. As we know, shame does not always look like shame. Consider the following list as it relates to the signs of shame in the therapeutic relationship.

Symptoms of Client Shame

— Loss of boundaries.
— Feeling judged, or judging others.
— Threats of termination.
— Others seen as "the enemy."
— Forgetting they are cared about.
— Competition: "If I were more like . . ."
— Superiority/inferiority swings.
— Shaming statements to self.
      "Why do I always . . ."
      "I never . . ."
      "I'm stupid, dumb, incompetent . . ."
      "If I wasn't so . . ."
— Shaming statements to others.
      "Why can't you ever . . ."
      "What's wrong with you?"
      "S/he is such a stupid . . ."
— Feelings of extreme self-consciousness.
— Striving for an excess of power.
— "Making others dead" or nonexistent as an expression.
— Feeling helpless and victimized.
— Feeling and expressing contempt for self, others, and the therapy process.
— Self-mutilation and other forms of self-abuse.
— Other self-destructive behaviors, including resuming substance abuse.

Counselors can also feel shameful as they deal with their clients. When feeling shameful, a counselor is more vulnerable to crossing boundaries. It is especially difficult for counselors to hold clients and colleagues accountable when feeling ashamed. It is common during these times for the counselor to take responsibility for others' boundary issues.

We might also need our clients at these times to convince us that we are good counselors, that we are making a difference. This is clearly not the job of our clients.

Symptoms of Counselor Shame

— Any of the signs noted under client symptoms.
— Not referring clients to other professionals.
— Not exposing therapeutic work due to a sense of inadequacy.
— Professional isolation.
— Rage at clients or colleagues.
— Taking responsibility for other's mistakes or issues.
— Inability to openly acknowledge own mistakes.
— Inability to "stand up" for self when necessary.

PROFESSIONAL BOUNDARY MODEL

Given that boundary dilemmas confront counselors daily, and that they often do not fall on the extreme end of the continuum, there is no guide for every situation that arises. It is, however, crucial to have a process of making decisions and exploring any therapeutic discomfort that may be present.

A model for working with boundary issues was developed by the author both for clinical work and for supervision purposes. It demonstrated the process by which a client or clinician can determine when boundaries are in question. Consider the following model:

```
     ┌ 1. CLIENT BEHAVIOR ------------- > 2. COUNSELOR FEELING RESPONSE ┐
   ┌─┘ 7                                                                 │
   └                                                                     ↘
5. FEEDBACK TO CLIENT <------4. CASE CONSULTATION <------3. COUNSELOR ASSESSMENT
                             — client behaviors           AND INITIAL RESPONSE
                             — counselor feelings
                               assessment
                               response and behaviors
```

Consider the following case example:

1. *Client Behavior* — A client walks into your office saying she needs to talk with you.

2. *Your Feelings* — You feel intruded upon and irritated. You also feel "caught" and embarrassed because you were reading the paper with your shoes off, and your feet up on the desk.

3. *Your Assessment and Initial Response* — Your assessment of the situation includes thinking that your client has some boundary problems (not knocking), and that she is in some kind of a crisis.

You ask your client to please knock in the future. You then talk with her but notice that during and after the session you are feeling uneasy. Your mind keeps returning to the client throughout the week.

4. *Case Consultation* — You talk about the situation in supervision. You identify that this client has continually crossed your boundaries, and that while you have set limits, her behavior has not changed substantially. You realize that you have been feeling resentful and withholding toward her. You also realize with the feedback from your supervisor and supervision group that you have not put the violations in terms of a framework of boundaries with your client. You now see that the boundary problems exhibited with you are like the boundary problems in her family of origin who she has been trying unsuccessfully to emancipate from. It becomes clear that you have been feeling in a continual state of shame with this client. You have not been very effective in your work with her or her family. As you talk about it further you realize that what you are feeling with her she is feeling with her family. This insight gives you a new perspective, and reduces the shame, as well as helps you choose a new course of action.

5. *Feedback to Client* — You meet with your client and talk about boundaries and boundary problems. You set firm limits, knowing that if they are crossed again you will model firm boundaries regardless of the crisis. You talk with your client about how hard it must be to set limits with her family. You ask her if she is willing to talk about her boundary issues in group to get feedback about how others respond to them. In this way your client may gain the insight that others respond as she does to intrusions.

Responding to Colleagues' Boundary Issues

Awareness of one's own sense of uneasiness and concern is of major importance when responding to colleagues as well as when responding to clients. Often when there has been exploitation of a client, co-workers report having a sense that something was not right with the offending counselor. It is important to verbalize concerns. This is a process which takes courage and commitment. It is more respectful and loyal to confront colleagues openly than to deny that they are in trouble. The structure of a supervision group allows for greater opportunity to confront boundary problems before they become violations.

Systemic Ethical and Boundary Considerations

Organizational Characteristics

Any program that is designed for a homogeneous population will be shaming to clients who don't "fit." For years treatment programs were set up for (and by) white men. Women and non-white clients were expected to fit even though they could not. The omission of lecture material that related to issues specific to women and minorities reinforced the shame of being different. The lack of role models with whom clients could relate also reinforced the lack of belonging. Many female clients report hearing group members speak derogatorily of women. Minority group members experience the same phenomenon with racist remarks, jokes and expressions.

If it is mandatory that clients have physical contact, it can be assumed that some are experiencing physical boundary violations as they then lose the power of choice. It is important to teach people that they have a right to say no to any physical contact which does not feel comfortable to them. They need to experience saying no without being punished or shamed for doing so. Many of our clients come from families where they were not in charge of their own bodies, where their feelings were not considered important. This requires that the structure of the treatment program differ from the structure of the family.

In an enmeshed organization the staff (and consequently the clients) are over-connected. Counselors and often the clients will be guilted and shamed for needing autonomy or for trying to emancipate from the system. The staff may work together, socialize together, and possibly enter into sexual relationships with each other. Other symptoms of an enmeshed organization include the hiring of ex-clients, or in extreme cases, current clients. Professional closure also occurs, in which staff members are not open to ideas or to professionals who are "outside" the program, resulting in rigidity of the program's ideology.

In a disengaged organization the staff (and consequently the clients) are neglected and neglectful. There is often a lack of accountability, with little support. Staff and clients may come and go with little attention, either formally or informally. Clients also become vulnerable within this structure as the staff may turn to them to make up for what is lacking organizationally.

It is essential that an organization have a clear set of guidelines regarding ethical practice. If a counselor exhibits poor boundaries with clients and colleagues and there is no formal policy, little protection is available for the clients or for the program.

Organizational Disrespect for Gender, Racial and Cultural Issues

For centuries women have been shamed for being women, for being different from men. Women have traditionally been defined by men and then were shamed both for failing to fit the definition and for fitting the definition. Historically, what is "male" has been more valued than what is "female." The exclusion of women as important individuals and as an important group is reflected in the use of male pronouns and references in academic literature. The media still fails to depict women in varied roles.

There is a double stigma to being a female alcoholic or drug addict. Society has failed to openly acknowledge that women are also vulnerable to substance abuse. Access to treatment has been extremely difficult for women due to lack of attention to their spatial needs such as child care, issues of oppression and powerlessness, polydrug abuse, and sexuality issues. In addition, it has been shown that the number of verbal responses exhibited in group are positively correlated with treatment success, and that women, when in group with men, show significantly fewer verbal responses (Nielsen & Koehler, 1980). This, among other data, seems to indicate that gender specific groups within treatment may serve women more effectively (Beckman, 1975, pp. 797-824; Curlee, 1970, pp. 239-247).

Any program designed by and for a homogeneous group will be inherently shaming for those who don't/can't fit the model. There is also a greater risk of boundary violations simply due to the counselor's level of cultural ignorance. When deciding what constitutes health a counselor and a program will exhibit cultural bias. The more balanced the staff the more balanced will be the treatment model.

Counselors need to be well educated multi-culturally and to be committed to learning what they do not know as the need arises. It is violating to expect clients to teach counselors or other clients about cultural or racial issues. It is also violating to stereotype a client. It is important for counselors not to assume that if they know about culture they know about all people, and vice-versa. Sensitivity to cultural issues include a recognition of difference among individuals.

TREATMENT RECOMMENDATIONS
FOR PROFESSIONAL BOUNDARY MAINTENANCE

For Counselors

1. Increase awareness of boundary vulnerabilities and on-going boundary issues with clients, taking into consideration type of client, agency, colleagues, etc.
2. Clearly set limits with clients and colleagues regarding:
   — Receiving calls at home — both from clients and colleagues.
   — Friendships with clients.
   — Confidentiality issues.
   — Personal questions from clients.
   — "Working harder" than the client.
   — Physical boundary issues.
3. Take vacations and sick time to provide renewal and re-energizing. A counselor will then be less likely to become "needy" with clients.
4. Attend workshops, trainings, etc. to avoid professional closure and rigidity.
5. Do personal therapy when needed.
6. Get personal and professional ego needs met separate from therapeutic work with clients.

7. Work only as many direct service hours as therapeutically manageable.
8. Obtain good clinical supervision, preferably within a group structure. Ideally, the supervisor is a consultant from outside the organization.
9. Pay due attention to boundary issues with colleagues.

For Administrators

1. Develop policies to help avoid serious boundary violations. Questions to consider include:
   — Can counselors develop friendships, or other types of relationships, with clients after the client terminates, and if so what is the mandatory length of time of termination before reassociation?
   — What are the consequences of hiring ex-clients? Weigh out the pros and cons to the client as well as to the program.
   — What are the rules about staff members being sexual with each other?
   — What are the consequences if the rules are broken?
2. Have staff members review organizational rules and ethics.
   — Encourage each staff member to brainstorm every possible exception to the rules.
   — Process any relevant information.
3. Always check references when hiring counselors.
4. Supply good clinical supervision for all staff members, preferably with an outside consultant.
5. Provide opportunities for staff development.
6. Require counselor self-care.
7. Explore any client complaints and see these through to completion (be able to say what they did and what did not happen).
8. Do not ignore early warning signals of ethical concerns.
9. Be consistent with rules and boundaries.
10. Help staff members leave as appropriate without guilting or shaming them for leaving the organization.

11. Provide a client bill of rights which includes appropriate behaviors for counselors and clients.
12. Ask clients about past counselors, specifically in terms of abuse.
13. Require adequate training of staff.
14. Provide training on personal and professional boundaries.

In conclusion, it is impossible to have a therapeutic relationship without struggling with boundary issues. These struggles can be extremely beneficial to clients. It is, however, our ethical responsibility to provide service with adequate knowledge and attention given to the inherent power of the relationship.

REFERENCES

Beckman, L. (1975). Women Alcoholics. *Journal of Alcohol Studies*, vol. 36, 7.

Coleman, E. & Colgan, P. (1986). Boundary Inadequacy in Drug Dependent Families. *Journal of Counseling and Development*.

Coleman, E. & Schaefer, S. (1986). Boundaries of Sex and Intimacy Between Client and Counselor. *Journal of Counseling and Development*, 64, 341-344.

Curlee, J. (1970). A Comparison of Male and Female Patients at an Alcoholism Treatment Center. *Journal of Psychology*, 74, 239-247.

Evans, S. & Schaefer, S. (in Press). Incest and Chemically Dependent Women: Treatment Considerations. *Alcoholism Treatment Quarterly*.

Kardener, S., Fuller, M. & Mensh, I. (1973). A Survey of Physicians' Attitudes and Practices Regarding Erotic and Non-erotic Contact With Patients. *American Journal of Psychiatry*, 130, 1077-1081.

Killorin, E. & Olson, D. (1980). Clinical Rating Scales For The Circumplex Model of Marital and Family Therapy. *Family Social Science*, University of MN.

Minuchin, S. (1974). Families and Family Therapy, Cambridge, MA: Harvard University Press.

Nielsen, L. (1984). Sexual Abuse and Chemical Dependency: Assessing the Risk For Adult Children. *Focus on Family*, Nov/Dec.

Nielsen, L., Peterson, M., Shapiro, M. & Thompson, P. (1986). Supervision Approaches In Cases of Boundary Violations and Sexual Victimization By Therapists. Minnesota Task Force on Sexual Exploitation by Counselors and Therapist Manual.

Nielsen, L. (1986). Personal and Professional Boundaries. *Oodel Homen's Treatment Project Program Manual*, (In Press).

Nielsen, L. & Kochler, S. (1980). Out-patient Counselors Attitudes Toward Women in Chemical Dependency Treatment. Research Paper presented at the 1981 National Conference on Sexuality and Chemical Dependency, Mpls. MN.

Peterson, M. (1986). Boundary Issues in Psychotherapy, Unpublished Paper.

Shapiro, R. (1977). A Family Therapy Approach To Alcoholism. *Journal of Marriage and Family Counseling*, October.

Schoener, G., Paper available through Walk-In Counseling, Minneapolis, MN.

Thompson, P., Shapiro, M., Nielsen, L. & Peterson, M. (1986). Supervision Strategies To Prevent Sexual Abuse of Clients By Therapists and Counselors. Minnesota Task Force on Sexual Exploitation by Counselors and Therapists Manual.

White, W. (1986). Incest in the Organizational Family, The Ecology of Burnout in Closed Systems. A Lighthouse Training Institute Publication.

Shame and Guilt Issues Among Women Alcoholics

Edith S. Lisansky Gomberg, PhD

SUMMARY. The author compares the experience of males and females with shame and guilt. Particular attention is given to the relation of these issues with alcoholism. Barriers to treatment are noted and the treatment of shame and guilt with women alcoholics is discussed.

A dictionary definition of shame and guilt (Webster, 1964) describes *shame* as a painful emotion produced by dishonor, disgrace, censure, or ". . . consciousness of guilt, shortcoming or impropriety in one's behavior." Shame is linked with humiliation, with the awareness of others that one is disgraced. *Guilt* is defined by the same dictionary as involving responsibility for an event, a feeling of culpability, a feeling of deserving punishment. While guilt feelings usually appear as, "I did wrong and I should make amends," guilt may escalate into what Webster's dictionary describes as, ". . . morbid self-reproach often manifested in marked preoccupation with the moral correctness of one's behavior." Guilt is a legal term: in American law, a person is presumed innocent until proved guilty. Guilt is also a religious term and one has only to look at James Joyce's "Portrait of the Artist as a Young Man" to see an example.

Kurtz (1981) uses a metaphor to define the difference between *shame* and *guilt*. If living is analogized to navigating a playing field, shame occurs when the navigator fails to achieve a goal. Guilt arises when the navigator goes out of bounds and steps over

Edith S. Lisansky Gomberg is Professor, School of Social Work, University of Michigan, Ann Arbor, MI 48109-1285.

the boundaries. Perceived failure produces shame and rule-breaking produces guilt.

Both of these affective responses may be linked to depression-fundamentally they are negative feelings. The emotional state linked to shame may be described as feelings of dysphoria, low self-regard, anger turned against the self, i.e., the feelings usually thought of as depressive symptomatology.

SOME COMMENTS ON SHAME

If shame involves positive identification with parental expectations, the falling short of such expectations and the consequent low self-esteem (Potter-Efron, 1987), a good case can be made for the existence of greater shame among women than among men in contemporary society. In spite of the feminist movement and in spite of an ever-increasing percentage of women in the work force, women are still socialized by parents and teachers (the conveyers of societal role prescriptions and proscriptions) to be primarily the *keepers of personal relationships*. Girls grow up to be women who are invested in establishing and maintaining personal relationships:

> . . . Women usually assume the responsibility for the emotional welfare and continuity of family members. They facilitate communication, they sooth interpersonal contusion and abrasion, they comfort, support, and heal. . . . (Gizynski, 1986, p. 3)

When they perceive themselves to be failing in this responsibility, women experience shame. Shame produces dysphoric feelings, i.e., depression, and there is overwhelming evidence that women manifest more depression than do men (Gove, 1979; Weissman & Klerman, 1979). This gender difference appears whether the sample being studied is an (assumed) normal sample of the general population in a community study or a clinical sample of people in treatment. Furthermore, also linked to the experience of shame, women consistently show lower self-esteem than do men and again this is true whether the people being studied are clinical patients or undergraduates.

The role of shame in women's lives reaches an apex in an anthropological study of the Gainj, a small preliterate tribe in Papua New Guinea (Johnson, 1981), The Gainj have one of the highest suicide rates in the world and the suicides occur disproportionately among women between 20 and 50. A Gainj woman explained to the anthropologist that suicide is, ". . . what a woman can do when she has too much shame because no one will take care of her." In each case recorded by Johnson, the woman committed suicide after a quarrel with another woman (co-wife, mother-in-law, etc) in which the husband champions the other woman's cause, or after being physically abused by the husband. It is shame for the woman's family of origin to take her back so, in the face of real social rejection, she is likely to commit suicide. One must understand the social system involved:

> . . . female suicide can be seen as growing out of a gender system that requires male dominance but that offers women in return a definite assurance of protection by dominant males . . . (Johnson, 1981, p. 333)

SOME COMMENTS ON GUILT

Guilt, it is theorized, is based on difficulties in impulse control and in rule-breaking behaviors. (This is complicated by the fact that many individuals who have difficulty in impulse control and who engage in rule-breaking behavior do not experience guilt; this is what has been called sociopathy, character disorder, psychopathic personality.) The epidemiology of disordered behavior indicates that there is more rule-breaking or deviant behaviors by men than by women (Gove, 1985). If the equation was simply, deviant behaviors — guilt, then statistically, guilt would be more characteristic of male response. But it is not that simple. Women do have difficulties in impulse control and they do engage in rule-breaking behaviors. Such behaviors cover a wide range from misbehaving in a classroom to murder. One of the well explored topics of women's studies has been the double standard of societal response to deviant behaviors manifested by women and by men (e.g., Rosenfield, 1982). There is a good deal of evidence that female deviant behavior is viewed with more disapproval than male deviant behavior; the question is — what is the effect of such disapproval on the experience of guilt?

Guilt may arise from at least two sources. Without any other person being aware of X's behavior, X may experience guilt from *internal* sources. The psychoanalysts describe guilt as a manifestation of superego response. Guilt may also arise from *external* sources: X may feel guilty because of disapproval, gossip, social rejection, and here it is difficult to distinguish from shame. It is speculation but we may hypothesize that men are more likely to experience guilt from internal sources, women from external sources.

GENDER DIFFERENCES

There has been a shift in the status of women and clearly it is true that the percentage of married-women-with-children who are now in the workforce has increased considerably over the last decades. This has not been accompanied by a major redistribution of domestic responsibilities and for most women, the primary responsibility of household management and childrearing remains theirs. Even in "Marxist" societies, women return home from the workplace to assume most of the domestic chores. While there are more men cooking, shopping, taking care of children than was true 25 years ago, the redistribution of domestic responsibility has been modest in size.

There are fundamental differences in the ways in which men and women respond to their environments. In large part, these differences may be biologically based (Rossi, 1985) although it has been demonstrated cross-culturally that socialization pressure in raising girls is primarily in the direction of responsibility and nurturant behaviors in most societies (Barry, Bacon & Child, 1957). In the same societies, boys are socialized more in the direction of achievement and self-reliance. In a more recent discussion, Gilligan (1982) has emphasized:

> . . . the evidence that women perceive and construe social reality differently from men and . . . these differences center around experiences of attachment and separation. Women's sense of integrity appears to be entwined with an ethic

of care, so that to see themselves as women is to see themselves in a relationship of connection . . . (Gilligan, 1982,
p. 171)

The same socialization processes which define the acceptable
range of male and female behaviors also define the acceptable
limits of *affective* response, degree and kind. There are social
rules which permit women to be depressed and permit men to act
out to a greater degree, and these rules manifest themselves in the
statistics we have about gender differences in depression and in
deviant behaviors.

With this background, we may speculate about the relationship
of assigned social role, attachment and separation, an ethic of
care, failure, shame, guilt and substance abuse among women.
There are several hypotheses which may be considered in exam-
ining these relationships.

GUILT, SHAME AND SUBSTANCE ABUSE

1. There are gender differences in the manifestations of
shame. Both sexes experience shame. Men may be disgusted
with themselves but are less likely to display depressive symptoms. Rather than turning their negative feelings toward themselves, they are more likely to *act out* in a variety of deviant
behaviors.

2. The statistics of suicide support a hypothesis about gender
differences in shame and guilt. Women are more likely than men
to *attempt* suicide (most frequently through overdosing) and the
attempts appear as a combination of depression (shame), impulsivity and anger. The most frequent suicide attempters are young
women alcoholics (Gomberg, 1986). But men commit suicide at
higher rates (and with more violent means) than women. While
suicide rates drop among aging women, suicide rates mount after
middle age for men, linked perhaps to depression (shame) over
loss of role.

3. Internalized shame is a critical concept among the antecedent conditions which preexist the development of alcoholism or
drug dependency among women. As an antecedent condition,
such internalized shame may be an important, even necessary

condition; shame, however, is not sufficient explanation of female alcoholism.

4. Internalized shame is experienced as depression, a state of dysphoric discomfort which leads to a search for relief. Substances are most frequently used and abused by women in a medicinal way, an attempt at self-cure, a behavior which accomplishes a temporary alleviation of psychic pain and an often accompanying feeling of self-confidence and energy. Women in Alcoholics Anonymous, reporting early symptoms of alcoholism, cite, ". . . personality change when drinking," and ". . . feeling more intelligent and capable when drinking," (James, 1975). The alcoholic men in the same study reported alcohol behaviors, e.g., increased tolerance, blackouts, sneaking and gulping drinks, as early symptoms.

5. Once heavy drinking or drug use has begun, the problem becomes circular. While the original motivation to drink was minimizing discomfort, the drinking bout only serves to produce, as an aftermath, more shame, more depression and heightened guilt (Marlatt, 1986). Being trapped in this circularity produces more depression so that the alcoholic woman makes a suicide attempt or, finding the depression unbearable, enters treatment (Gomberg, in preparation).

6. The onset of alcohol and drug problems are linked not only to internalized shame and the search for a mood modifier but also to difficulties experienced with *impulse control*. Although women are probably socialized toward more control of impulsivity than are men, some women do have problems with impulsivity (Jones, 1971; Gomberg, 1986) and these problems contribute to the rule-breaking behavior of heavy drinking or drug use. The impulsivity and the rule-breaking behaviors, in term, contribute to the intensification of guilt feelings. As the drinking bouts continue, the guilt mounts.

7. Women who are drinking heavily attach their guilt feelings to their perception of failure in assigned role behaviors. They perceive themselves as failed mothers (Finkelstein et al., 1981), failed wives (Gomberg, 1974), failed workers. Guilt about failure as mother is particularly singled out for reinforcement by the health care community (as well as the whole society) and the vast literature on fetal damage increases such guilt. There is also a

literature in alcohol studies which hypothesizes that alcoholism in the mother is more destructive within the family than is alcoholism in the father; research results are not really clear on this question.

SHAME, GUILT AND TREATMENT

When a patient enters treatment, he/she will present a clinical picture characterized by both shame and guilt. How to differentiate the *antecedent* from the *consequent* is a question to be posed about a variety of behaviors, states and moods the patient presents. This is not really an academic question: some of the consequences of alcoholism may be reversed, e.g., the body may recover and relationships may be restored when the person achieves lasting sobriety. But the self-view which preexisted the alcoholism, the psychic pain associated with shame and feelings of deprivation, and the repressed anger do not heal as quickly. The achievement of a more adaptive level of existence will involve coming to terms with a view of self and recovering from old psychic wounds, and that is a reeducation process, a resocialization process if you will, where learning takes place and where the patient comprehends that his/her pain was not really minimized but only intensified by alcohol/drug use. The process may be sequential: sobriety, physical recovery, restoration of social networks, resocialization.

Women who develop alcoholism, particularly those for whom onset occurs in their late twenties, thirties, early forties, are often women who have grown increasingly depressed and weary of the nurturant role. This may occur because they set standards of nurturing perfection, i.e., they must be the perfect wife, the perfect mother, the perfect adult child of needful parents. For many women in their twenties and thirties, there is the phenomenon of "superwoman," the woman who has a successful career and also comes home at night to be a superb wife, mother, homemaker. (The term "quality time" to describe the time such women spend with their children is a defensive ploy; since she spends less time with her children than does the housewife, the time should be "quality time.") Here the therapeutic maneuver must be toward the acceptance of being merely human. Someplace between "superwoman'' and the narcissistic abandonment of the nurturing role (''doing your own thing''), there is a middle ground: doing the best one can, accepting one's own limits, doing for others without paying too heavy a price, doing for oneself without abandoning others' needs. There is more clinical experience with the middle-aged alcoholic woman, often a housewife, who is disappointed with her life. For her, the feminist movement has contributed a great deal, and to help such a woman rebuild her life with new interests and even a new career has been generally accepted as part of the therapeutic process.

TREATMENT OF ALCOHOLIC WOMEN: SHAME

In a study of internalized shame, Cook (1987) has noted that for men, internalized shame and problems in the family of origin are both good predictors of adult emotional problems and addiction. For women, however, internalized shame is the significant predictor, and Cook offers the explanation that for women, difficulties in the family of origin are more readily converted or internalized into feelings of shame. Related to this point is a frequent theme in alcoholism literature: in clinical populations, female alcoholics almost always report more alcoholism in the family of origin than do male alcoholics (Gomberg, 1980). The reported rates of alcoholism as higher in the families of women than men alcoholics also appears in reviews (Armor, Polich & Stambul, 1978; Cotton, 1979) and in a recent comparison of professional persons who are members of Alcoholics Anonymous (Bissell & Haberman, 1984). In the Bissell and Haberman study, 29% of the men and 41% of the women report having at least one alcoholic parent. There is a good case to be made for reasoning that since there is more alcoholism in the families of origin reported by alcoholic women than by alcoholic men or by nonalcoholic women (Gomberg, 1986), there will also be a greater degree of shame.

Barriers to Treatment

First, as Potter-Efron (1987) has pointed out, shame inhibits expression and the impairment in functioning produced by shame begins to lessen only when shame is exposed to others ''in a safe environment.'' Women, being greater bearers of shame, are indeed inhibited in expressing these feelings, and it takes a good deal of trust in the therapist, before a woman alcoholic feels free to express these feelings.

The *second barrier* is one which is discussed all too infrequently in connection with female alcoholism: the anger or rage which simmers beneath the surface of many alcoholic women (Gomberg, 1976; Gomberg, 1981). Defenses against strong feelings of shame include the perfectionism discussed above and the feelings of rage. But expression of overt anger and resentment is not acceptable and it may be difficult for the alcoholic woman in treatment to express and ventilate such feelings.

A *third barrier* may reside not within the woman in treatment but within the therapist. It has been repeated many times but bears repeating again: the therapist needs to examine his/her own attitudes toward female deviance and to approach the woman alcoholic with acceptance. Only when the therapist can accept the person while rejecting the alcoholic behavior does treatment really work.

Finally, it should be noted that problems within the family system must be dealt with. Gilligan's (1982) phrasing, ''. . . to see themselves as women is to see themselves in a relationship of connection,'' says it very well. It is well-known that one of the most significant barriers to the treatment of women alcoholics lies in the complex motivation of spouse, parents, siblings, child, and other family members and close friends. Significant others may facilitate the therapeutic process or they may undo the progress made in treatment. Significantly more than men, women live in their social contexts and the social environment will act as reinforcer or dampener of the treatment process.

Some Steps in Treatment

For alcoholics with considerable burdens of shame, the open acknowledgement of such feelings is an essential part of the therapeutic process. For this reason among others, it is wise to offer both individual and group therapy. For some women, expression of shame feelings may come more readily in the one-to-one situation while for others, it may be easier in a small group of women who are able to facilitate each others' expression of such feelings. There has never been agreement as to whether women benefited more from group therapy or from one-to-one relationships although some have argued for the greater effectiveness of the latter (Pemberton, 1967; Curlee, 1971).

In addition to the acknowledgement of shame feelings, an essential component of the rehabilitative process is the shift in self-perception, the acceptance of self. With the preonset and alcoholic history the woman patient brings to the therapeutic encounter, she feels — and society supports that feeling — a failure. It takes a good deal of patient reassurance, support, acceptance (and work with the family) to help the shift in self-perception. For the therapist, a delicate balance must be maintained in which drinking relapses, broken appointments and tantrums are clearly not acceptable behaviors while the reassurance and emotional support is maintained. When the limits are tested (and they will be), it is a situation akin to the childrearing experience in which the child's misbehavior is disapproved while the child remains assured that he/she is loved.

Most alcoholic women who enter treatment facilities are of average and even above average intelligence. They are capable of understanding circularity and the futility of the vicious cycle in which they are embedded. Looking to alcohol to assuage feelings of shame, they have accumulated *more* shame (and guilt) by repeated drinking, and then attempted to assuage the shame and guilt by more drinking, and so on. There is no way to break into the circle of cause-and-effect, shame-and-drinking-and-shame without sobriety. Since the woman has usually come to the facility in a state of despair, she is ready to give up drinking — so she feels and so she says. But it is more difficult to understand and deal with the internalized shame and there will be no break in the circularity until the drinking stops. She is not able to deal with the forces that produce another drinking bout until she is in a sober state. Here it may be useful to borrow from the cognitive therapies the search for cues which trigger drinking bouts.

TREATMENT OF ALCOHOLIC WOMEN: GUILT

If guilt is the state that reminds the person that he/she must obey the norms or be punished, women may be seen as greater transgressors than men: (a) the socialization process emphasizes for them more than it does for the male that they are charged with the "law and order" responsibility of maintaining the norms, and (b) rule-breaking by women is viewed more negatively than rule-breaking by men (Knupfer, 1968; Rosenfield, 1982). A differentiation has been made between rational guilt and irrational guilt, and these may be viewed as reality-based guilt and omnipotence-based guilt. Guilt is irrational and neurotic when the person assumes that his/her acts or thoughts are the pivotal point around which other peoples' acts and other peoples' troubles develop. To assume that all the bad things that happen within a family are "my fault" is an illusion of power to control events. In the therapeutic process, a distinction needs to be made between these different guilts; rational guilt can be faced and dealt with through sobriety, restitution, etc. Dealing with rational guilt is built into the structure of Alcoholics Anonymous. In the treatment situation, dealing with irrational guilt is more of a process of uncovering, facing, working through.

Although there are many different situation-specific guilts, we will discuss "alcoholism guilt," anguish associated with a woman's alcoholic career. Women, enmeshed in networks of nurturance and responsibility, will have guilt feelings *before* the onset of alcoholism but once involved in the alcoholic cycle, the load of guilt increases immeasurably. The indignity of intoxication, acts committed while under the influence, the failure of performance in interpersonal obligations, in vino veritas tantrums, falling short in primary role relationships — all contribute to a heavy load with which most women begin the treatment process. Interestingly enough, in James' (1975) interviews with members of Alcoholics Anonymous, male alcoholics mentioned feeling guilty about drinking as an *early* stage of alcoholism but the women alcoholics placed guilt feelings about drinking as a *middle* stage. It is only, so to speak, after the heavy drinking has been going on for some time that the women participants in the study report feeling guilty about their drinking.

There are social pressures which intensify the discomfort of guilt feelings among alcoholic women. Although many women with drinking problems maintain sobriety during a pregnancy, they are inundated with the message that their drinking harms the fetus (even the comfort of remaining sober during pregnancy is eroded because scientists inform them that having drunk heavily *before* becoming pregnant might have damaging fetal effects). There is also the perception and common belief that maternal alcoholism has "worse" effects on the children than paternal alcoholism; in spite of the ambiguity of the evidence, this is stated often and strongly. Marital disruption rates of the women seen in treatment facilities are significantly higher than the marital disruption rates of the men seen in the same facilities and instead of viewing this as a greater load of stigma and rejection and an unwillingness of nonalcoholic males to be supportive, it is sometimes cited as more proof that alcoholic women are "worse." There are several reports in the literature that women alcoholics (and women narcotic addicts, women schizophrenics, etc) are "poorer patients," usually defined as noisier, more rebellious, and more demanding. And there is the widespread belief that women who enter treatment have poorer prognosis than men who enter treatment, although the evidence is sparse and there is little support for significant gender differences in recovery (Annis & Liban, 1980).

An examination of one of these charges: maternal alcoholism has more destructive effects on children than paternal alcoholism, shows mixed evidence. Some studies suggest that alcoholic women are *guilty as charged*. Cork (1969) reported that the children she interviewed expressed more negative views of alcoholic mothers than of alcoholic fathers. Krauthamer (1979) found alcoholic mothers displaying more ambivalent, confused and inconsistent behavior toward their children than matched nonalcoholic mothers but concluded that this was a consequence of the drinking and was reversible with sobriety. Williams (1982) found that children in households headed by alcoholic mothers, low in income and job skills, were more neglected than children in families where the father was alcoholic and a nonalcoholic mother served as primary caregiver. Obviously the effect of one parent's alcoholism can be minimized if there is a stable, nonalcoholic parent present, and the higher rate of marital disruption among women alcoholics suggests that they must struggle as single-parent households to a greater extent than do male alcoholics.

There are some reports which present a rather different view.

McLachlan, Walderman and Thomas (1973) compared teenagers in intact families, alcoholic and nonalcoholic and found that adolescents with alcoholic mothers view those mothers as inept but they regard recovered mothers with real admiration. El-Guebaly, Offord, Sullivan and Lynch (1978) compared children of parents diagnosed as alcoholic, schizophrenic or depressed; no significant differences were found in the adjustment of children with an ill father or an ill mother. And Bromet and Moos (1977) compared 23 families in which the wife was alcoholic with 23 matched families in which the husband was the alcoholic. They report,

> . . . There were no significant differences in the family environments between the two groups of alcoholic families. Nor were there any differences in the perceptions of wives (or) husbands . . . or children of alcoholic mothers compared with children of alcoholic fathers . . . The present study failed to support a hypothesis about more negative social environment in families with alcoholic wives. (Bromet & Moos, 1977, p. 335)

Obviously the research literature is not going to offer a clear answer to the question whether an alcoholic mother is more damaging to the children in the family than an alcoholic father. But clearly, alcoholism in the family while the child is growing up is damaging. How far does a therapist go in allaying a woman alcoholic's guilty feelings?

Somewhere between the position that "no harm has been done," and the position that "you sinned and *should* feel guilty," there lies a therapeutic position that what is done cannot be recalled but it can be remedied, that the inconsistency and unpredictability of behavior produced by the drinking can be changed, that sobriety is the first step toward reorganizing role behaviors. Whether the woman alcoholic has been a "bad" mother, wife, daughter, sister during the period of her heavy drinking is history now but guilt is treatable and recovery is possible. The reality-based guilts are probably best dealt with in a period of sobriety in which obligations can be met in a reasonable way. There is always the possibility, to be discussed with the patient, that with sobriety, she will overdo the restitution and begin feeling resentful and put upon. Moderation in restitution is a good way to go.

The irrational guilts, rooted in early life experience, can be examined and worked through only after rapport and trust has developed between therapist and patient. The irrational guilts are closely tied to internalized shame and surface only when the patient feels safe. Ambivalent feelings, perceptions of childhood deprivations, angers, resentments will gradually emerge. The illusion of omnipotence will surface and the woman alcoholic needs to recognize that there have been bad events for which she has, irrationally, assumed responsibility. The neurotic need for punishment and obsessive rumination over bad deed needs to be differentiated from reality-based consequences of the woman's drinking.

What to do with the unfairness with which women alcoholics are treated? This unfairness is part of the double standard which is an unfortunate fact of life. Support, sympathy and understanding are appropriate (and the therapist need not necessarily be a woman). Life is not always "fair," and the woman alcoholic needs to confront the unfairness and come to terms with it. Handwringing and maudlin sentiments are not helpful. The question is what the woman alcoholic wants to do with the rest of her life. Some women may want to be feminist activists in one way or another, other women may want to return to a traditional female role (if they have that choice), and still others may want to search for a balance between feminism and traditional role obligations and satisfactions.

The goals of therapy are not to terminate treatment with a patient in whom guilt is absent. The goal is to reduce guilty feelings to manageability, to deal with reality-based guilts directly, and to work through as much of the irrational guilt as necessary to reach an equilibrium.

POSTSCRIPT

Alcoholic patients, in spite of their common symptomatology, are not a homogeneous group, and there have been a wide variety of typologies expounded. Variability may exist in character traits, in coping mechanisms, in life styles. in psychiatric symptomatology. Clearly, there is variability among women alcoholics in demographic features: they vary by social class, by race, by age, by sexual orientation, by current marital and employment status, by positive or negative family history of alcoholism, and even by preferred-drugs-other-than-alcohol. To speak of shame and guilt as manifested by "the alcoholic woman" is permissible only if we note that there are great differences among alcoholic women in the degree to which and in the style in which these states of mind manifest themselves.

This discussion has dealt with the manifestations of shame and guilt and therapists' response to them. These are critical components of the psychotherapeutic process. One must not, however, overfocus on the process to the exclusion of other essential components of the treatment process. Dealing with the health status and need for adequate diet and exercise regime, concern with significant others in conjoint and family therapy, rehabilitation of a marriage that might be saved through marital counseling, diagnosis and treatment of children who show emotional problems, sexual therapies, even vocational guidance and help in returning to school or a job—all are essential. Construction or reconstruction of social networks is critical. One cannot separate the process of dealing with shame and guilt and the rehabilitation of many other features of a woman's life.

REFERENCES

Annis, H. M. & Liban. C. B. "Alcoholism in Women: Treatment Modalities and Outcomes," In: O. J. Kalant (ed.), *Alcohol and Drug Problems in Women*, Research Advances in Alcohol and Drug Problems. NY: Plenum Press, Volume 5, 1980.

Armor, D. J., Polich, J. M. & Stambul, H. B., *Alcoholism and Treatment*, NY: Wiley, 1978.

Barry, H., Bacon, M. K. & Child, I. L., "A Cross-Cultural Survey of Some Sex Differences in Socialization," *Journal of Abnormal and Social Psychology*, Vol. 55, No. 3, pp. 327-332, 1958.

Bissell, L. & Haberman, P. W., "Alcoholism in the Professions: Follow-up Sobriety and Relapses," *Alcoholism Treatment Quarterly*, Vol. 2, No. 2, 1985.

Bromet, E. & Moos, R. H., "Environmental Resources and the Posttreatment Functioning of Alcoholic Patients," *Journal of Health and Social Behavior*, Vol. 18, No. 3, pp. 326-338, 1977.

Cook, D. "Measuring Shame," *Alcoholism Treatment Quarterly*, Vol. 4, No. 2, pp. in this volume. 1987.

Cork, R. M. "The Forgotten Children: a Study of Children with Alcoholic Parents," Toronto, Ontario: Paperjacks. 1969.

Cotton, N. S., "The Familial Incidence of Alcoholism: A Review," *Journal of Studies on Alcohol*, Vol. 40, No. 1, pp. 89-116.

Curlee, J., "Sex Differences in Patient Attitudes Toward Alcoholism Therapy," *Quarterly Journal of Studies on Alcohol*, Vol. 32, 1971, pp. 643-650.

el-Guebaly, N., Offord, D. R., Sullivan, K. T. & Lynch, G. W., "Psychosocial Adjustment of the Offspring of Psychiatric Inpatients: The Effect of Alcoholic, Depressive, and Schizophrenic Parentage," *Canadian Psychiatric Association Journal*, Vol. 23, No. 5, 1978, pp. 281-290.

Finkelstein, N., Brown, K-A N. & Laham, C. W., Alcoholic mothers and guilts: Issues for Caregivers, *Alcohol Health and Research World*, Vol. 6, No. 1, 1981, pp. 45-49.

Gilligan, C., *In a Different Voice: Psychological Theory and Women's Development*, Cambridge, MA; Harvard University Press, 1982.

Gizynski, M., *Women and Depression*, Mimeographed, 4 pp.

Gomberg, E. S. L., "Women and Alcoholism," In: V. Franks & V. Burtle (eds.), *Women in Therapy*, NY: Brunner/Mazel, 1974, pp. 169-190.

Gomberg, E. S. L., "The female alcoholic," In: R. E. Tarter & A. A. Sugerman (eds.), *Alcoholism: Interdisciplinary Approaches to an Enduring Problem*, Reading, MA: Addison Wesley, 1976, pp. 603-636.

Gomberg, E.S.L., "Risk Factors Related to Alcohol Problems among Woman: Proneness and Vulnerability, "*Research Monograph No. 1 Alcoholism and Alcohol Abuse among Women, Research Issues*, National Institute on Alcohol Abuse and Alcoholism, DHEW (ADM) 1980, pp. 80-835, 83-120.

Gomberg, E. S. L., "Women and Alcoholism: Psychosocial Issues," *Research Monograph No. 16. Women and Alcohol: Health Related Issues*, National Institute on Alcohol Abuse and Alcoholism, DHHS (ADM) 1986, pp. 86-1139, 78-120.

Gomberg, E. S. L., Alcoholic Women's Reasons for Entering Treatment, Forthcoming.

Gove, W. R., "Sex Differences in the Epidemiology of Mental Disorder: Evidence and Explanations," In: E. S. Gomberg & V. Franks (eds.) *Gender and Disordered Behavior*, NY: Brunner-Mazel, 1979, pp. 23-68.

Gove, W. R., "The Effect of Age and Gender on Deviant Behavior: a Biopsychosocial Perspective, "In: A. S. Rossi (ed.) *Gender and the Life Course*, NY: Aldine 1985, pp. 115-144.

James, J. E., "Symptoms of Alcoholism in Women: A Preliminary Study of A. A. Members, *Journal of Studies on Alcohol*, Vol. 36, 1975, pp. 1564-1569.

Johnson, P. L., "When Dying is Better Than Living: Female Suicide Among the Gainj of Papua New Guinea," *Ethnology*, Vol. 20, 1981, pp. 325-334.

Jones, M. C., "Personality Antecedents and Correlates of Drinking Patterns in Women," *Journal of Consulting and Clinical Psychology*, Vol. 36, 1971, pp. 61-69.

Knupfer, G., "Female Drinking Patterns," *Selected Papers Presented at the 15th Annual Meeting of the North American Association of Alcoholism Programs*, Washington, D.C., 1964, pp. 140-160.

Krauthamer, C., "Maternal Attitudes of Alcoholic and Nonalcoholics Upper Middle Class Women," *International Journal of the Addictions*, Vol. 14, 1979, pp. 639-644.

Kurtz, E., *Shame and Guilt: Characteristics of the Dependency Cycle*, Professional Education 7, Hazelden Foundation, 1981.

Marlatt, G. A., "Sex Differences in Psychosocial Alcohol Research: Implications for

Prevention," *Research Monograph No. 16, Women and Alcohol: Health-Related Issues*, National Institute on Alcohol Abuse and Alcoholism, DHHS, (ADM), 1986, pp. 86-1139, 260-271.

McLachlan, J. F. C., Walderman, R. L. & Thomas, S., *A Study of Teenagers With Alcoholic Parents*, Research Monograph N. 3. Toronto: Donwood Institute, 1973.

Pemberton, D. A., "A Comparison of the Outcome of Treatment in Male and Female Alcoholics," *British Journal of Psychiatry*, Vol. 113, 1967, pp. 367-373.

Potter-Efron, R. T., "Shame and Guilt: Definitions, Processes and Treatment Issues with AODA Clients," *Alcoholism Quarterly*, Vol. 4, Number 2, 1987, pp. in this volume.

Rosenfield, S., "Sex Roles and Societal Reactions to Mental Illnesses: The Labeling of 'Deviant,' Deviance," *Journal of Health and Social Behavior*, Vol. 23, 1982, pp. 18-24.

Rossi, A. S., "Gender and Parenthood," In A. S. Rossi (ed.) *Gender and the Life Course*, NY: Aldine, 1985, pp. 161-191.

Webster's Third New International Dictionary of the English Language, Unabridged, Springfield, MA: G. & C. Merriam Co., 1964.

Weissman, M. M. & Klerman, G. L., "Sex Differences and the Epidemiology of Depression," In: E. S. Gomberg & V. Franks (eds.), *Gender and Disordered Behavior*, NY: Brunner/Mazel, 1979, pp. 381-425.

Williams, C. N. Differences in Child Care Practices among Families with Alcoholic Fathers, Alcoholic Mothers, and Two Alcoholic Parents, Doctoral Dissertation, Florence Heller Graduate School, Brandeis University.

Shame, Boundaries and Dissociation in Chemically Dependent, Abusive and Incestuous Families

Sue Evans, MA, CCDP

SUMMARY. The goal of this article is to draw from the integrate concepts from a number of schools of thought (chemical dependency, ego/developmental psychology, family systems approach, psychoanalysis, and feminist therapy) into a cohesive whole in an attempt to increase understanding of how shame impacts individuals who grew up in highly dysfunctional systems. The following paragraph is an overview of the literature that proceeds the discussion in this article.

Numerous authors have identified developmental phases that children experience in the formation of their identity (Erikson, Kaplan, Mahler). Development is defined as the progressive changes in the "meaning making ability" of the person as they proceed through these developmental phases. The child's "meaning making ability" is the perception of him/herself in the world and how s/he makes sense out of it. Within this process, boundary development/maintenance has proven to be an integral part of identity formation. The process of separation/individualization is paramount in the development of health boundaries. Briefly, separation/individuation is a developmental stage, whereby the child proceeds from a symbiotic relationship (delusion of a common boundary) with parenting figures through a progressive development towards a fully differentiated personality. Without boundaries one can not begin to foster a positive identity *or* healthy expressions of intimacy (Erickson, Hammer, Mahler). Important differences between males and females have been explored with females having been found to have much greater difficulty in the

---

Sue Evans is in private practice in Minneapolis, MN.

separation/individuation process (Chowdrow, Hammer). Other authors have clearly laid out the consequences to identity when shame (common to alcoholic families) interferes with this developmental process (Brown, Kaufman, Kopp, Miller). In chemically dependent families, boundary problems such as neglect and/or enmeshment interfere with a healthy identity (Brown, Coleman & Colgan, Nielsen). It is becoming increasingly clear that there is a correlation between intimacy/dysfunction and chemically dependent families (Coleman, Brown).

The following article carries this discussion further by exploring how boundaries get violated, the resulting consequences to identity, the function of dissociation, differences between male and female socialization and therapeutic models for recovery.

BOUNDARY VIOLATIONS

Emotional Boundary Violations

Identity formation is a developmental phenomenon. Identity refers to an individual's sense of self, one's self-concept of having worth, feelings of adequacy and dignity as a human being. This identity interprets the meaning of one's world and perceptions. Identity formation hinges upon the appropriate development of boundaries as a means of defining identity.

It is helpful to think about boundaries as a psychic bubble that surrounds each of us, a bubble that helps separate us from each other. Boundaries evolve as the child continues through the stages of development, defined usually by the age of three years. "Boundaries define our space like our personal territory. One physical boundary is our skin. It separates our insides from our outsides. We also have psychological boundaries. Although invisible, they are equally important. They keep us separate from other people, protect our individuality and our differentness from other people" (Ellis).

From birth to six months of age, the child is a physiological creature, (eating, sleeping, breathing, etc.) typically in a symbiotic relationship with the parent, totally dependent. The psychic bubble includes the parent at this phase of development.

Six months to three years is an extremely important time for the child to develop boundaries/identity through the separation/individuation process (Erickson, Kaplan, Mahler, Miller). As the child develops physiologically and neurologically it is beginning to discern its separateness from the parent. The psychic bubble has permeable boundaries but it begins to surround just the child. Parents need to allow the child to have attachment *to* and independence *from* themselves in order for the child to complete this separation task. If the separation/individuation process is interfered with by intrusion, such as parental narcissism, psychopathology, overprotectiveness, or disrespected privacy, boundary problems can occur (Mahler, Masterson, Miller, Hammer).

The following is an example of emotional intrusions in the parent/child relationship: Mom feels very insecure about her skills as a parent. She interprets the child's behavior as a direct reflection of her. She therefore acts very controlling as she needs her child to be perfect so that she can feel adequate. She may come to demand that the child never cry, misbehave or get dirty. Her needs therefore become primary. The child is valued for what s/he can give to the parent. Shame is induced in the child by never being able to live up to these unreasonable expectations.

Intrusive bonding with the parent can occur in a number of ways. Stierlin and Ravenscroft (1972) suggest that a family member may be bound to a parent in one of three ways. On one level the parent can infantalize and spoil the child into a compliancy and submissiveness sufficient to prevent the child from differentiating. On a second level, the parent can bind the child by interfering with the ability to express independent needs, motives, and goals. On a third level, the parent can bind the child through massive conscious and unconscious uses of loyalty demands and shaming (Brown).

Boundary invasions can cause one to feel invaded and hopelessly bound to the family. This can cause the intense pain and co-dependent behaviors often observed in chemically dependent families. An example of this is the child who feels responsible and hides mom's bottle in an attempt to control her chemical use. The author is suggesting that in some cases this role reversal begins before the child can even speak.

It is important to put this into the context of systemic family dynamics. This role reversal can not simply be reduced to the child's caretaking or the parent's unreasonable expectations of the child. It involves a whole system of family rules, expectations and roles which impact the child's connection to the family, which in turn impacts the child's ability to maintain and formulate boundaries.

The resulting role reversals, co-dependent behaviors and blurring of generational lines are all consequences of emotional boundary violations common to chemically dependent families. Other ways in which families intrude on emotional boundaries are: parent figures pick out the children's clothes/friends, make their decisions for them, read their diary/mail, listen in on private conversations, expect to be told all their secrets, expect them to be their main confidant (emotional marriage to one of the parents) and basically have an over-investment in their achievements.

Beyond intrusive parenting practices, boundaries can also be negatively affected by neglectful parenting. If parents are unavailable or rejecting of their children, shame is induced in children by the lacking of a relationship. Kaufman (1980) suggests that a breaking of the interpersonal bridge is the basis of a shame-based identity. If children's needs are ignored or attended to inconsistently, (i.e., Dad is too drunk some days to notice) eventually children can feel that *they* are bad because they needed something from the parent. They interpret not getting their needs met as that *they* are not worthy. Their identity is then formed around the myth of them being bad (Kaufman). "Dad would love me if I was lovable."

In that parents are the most important relationships (for better or for worse) that children have, their very survival depends on making sure those relationships are maintained. Children will do almost anything to survive, even blame themselves if there is trouble in the family. They will even pretend to be someone else if who they are is unacceptable (Winnocott's False-Self/Kopp's Mask).

Children identify with those who are important to them. Introjection occurs when they identify with significant others in their lives and internalize that image as a part of themselves (Klein). This, for instance, can occur when parents are very shaming to their children (Watkins & Watkins). They internalize an image of the shaming parent and it becomes a part of their identity. Their identity is then formulated around a shame-based system. Shame is a reaction to inappropriate/conflicting family rules, roles and expectations.

Boundary development can therefore be interfered with by either intrusive or neglectful parenting techniques. "In enmeshed families autonomy needs were neglected. In disengaged families dependency needs were neglected" (Neilsen).

Physical Boundary Violations

Physical abuse is, of course, a physical boundary violation. More subtle examples of physical violations may include the following: unwanted touch, being held down against their will, or being poked and tickled until they cry. It teaches children that they have no rights or control over their own bodies. A child who is regularly intruded upon physically doesn't ever learn that s/he can say no.

The neglect issue of lack of affectional touch might also be viewed as a physical boundary issue. While not involving intrusion, per se, touch deprivation is often as shame producing as physical violations to the child. "There must be something wrong with me if Dad doesn't want to touch me." In that affectional touch is a human necessity, this also makes the child more vulnerable and at risk for abuse as the child seeks elsewhere to get these touch needs met.

Sexual Boundary Violations

Sexual boundary violations are one more step along the continuum of boundary violations. Sexual boundary violations involve using the child for adult sexual gratification. Sexual abuse is, of course, highly traumatizing but so too is the threat of abuse (covert incest). If a professional rescued a child that they knew would be molested by a family member in five minutes, most of the damage would have already occurred. Damage from boundary violations, inappropriate expectations and emotional intrusions would have already taken place. Fear of molestation can be as damaging as overt abuse as it adds an insidious element of ambiguity which often contributes to a feeling of shame and craziness.

Table I explores the continuum of intrusion that occurs in families. It was developed by Susan Schaefer and modified by her

TABLE I
INCEST CONTINUUM: FAMILY DYNAMICS

INCEST PRECURSORS		COVERT INCEST	OVERT INCEST
EMOTIONAL BOUNDARY VIOLATIONS	PHYSICAL BOUNDARY VIOLATIONS		
Blurring of generational lines	Adult preoccupied with child's body/ bodily functions	Inadvertant touch	French kissing
Role reversal		Household Voyeurism	Exhibitionism
Parent's needs primary	Overly strict house- hold dress code	Physical punishment while naked	Fondling
Unmet dependency needs	Excessive tickling	Sexual hugs	Fellatio
			Cunnilingus
Closed system	Physical restraint against will for power needs	Ridicule of developing bodies	Penetration w/objects
Enmeshment/ disengagement	Parent demands physical comfort from child	Putting adult, sexual interpretation on child's behavior	Intercourse
Neglect	Touch deprivation	Lewd reading/video watching w/child	Sodomy
Overinvestment in child's achievements	Physical abuse	Use of objectifying, sexualizing language	
Intrusions w/child's decision-making		Invasive hygienic practices	
Telling child inappropriate secrets			
Disrespected privacy needs		*Authors wish to acknowledge the contributions of Lindsay Nielsen.	
Shame-based system			
Power dynamics		@ Oct. 1986 Schaefer and Evans	
Emotional abuse			

and the author. From a therapeutic standpoint, incest might best be viewed along a boundary violation continuum consisting of emotional boundary violations, physical boundary violations, covert incest and overt incest. (The continuum runs horizontal, examples of intrusions run vertical.) Emotional and physical boundary violations consist of family dynamics which serve as precursors to the actual incestuous behavior. Emotional boundary violations are characterized by family dynamics in which enmeshment, boundary ambiguity and identity diffusion are prominent features. Physical boundary violations occur when one's body is disrespected, neglected or when one experiences physical intrusions. Covert incest occurs when these underlying dynamics combine with an intended or felt sexual connotation or interpretation. Blatant sexual contact and/or penetration identifies overt incest.

Note the far left hand column. These characteristics are very common in alcoholic families. If the family rules allow for emotional and/or physical boundary violations, they are at risk for incestuous behavior. The families that fit along this continuum share many boundary violations in common. If a family has experienced overt or covert incest, they have also experienced some emotional/physical boundary violations too. This model offers an explanation for why there is such a high correlation between chemically dependent and incestuous families.

EFFECTS OF BOUNDARY VIOLATIONS

If a child has had his/her boundaries violated, whether emotionally, physically or sexually, there can be some common effects: boundary ambiguity, crisis orientation, assuming the victim role, having issues with touch, fear of intimacy/fear of abandonment and a shame-based identity.

Boundary Ambiguity

Boundary ambiguity is having an unclear sense of one's own boundaries. It is not knowing where one's own parameters are, where one's responsibilities end or how to go about keeping the integrity of one s identity. If children have had their boundaries violated, they have learned that to ask is to be turned down, to be needy is to be shameful, the value of themselves is in caretaking others and to mistrust their own needs, feelings or reality. This is early training for co-dependent behaviors.

Crisis Orientation

In chaotic, abusive or neglectful family systems, as most family members are emotionally depleted, needs typically go unattended to until they reach crisis proportions. At this point the family may rally around in support of the family member in crisis until this becomes unbearably close and intimate. People then find themselves looking for ways to increase the interpersonal distance. Shame is one product of dysfunctional reactions to family crises in that some people use shaming techniques to push other family members away.

Victim Role

In families with boundary problems, power gets perverted. Individuals don't experience a sense of personal power but rather one of either being overpowered or powering over someone else. "Deeds of violence are performed largely by those trying to establish their self-esteem, to defend their self-image and to demonstrate that they too are significant" (May).

One common response to severe boundary violations is assuming the victim role. This is learned behavior. While the abuse itself is damaging, assuming the victim role is much more destructive. It involves a whole way of life, that of assuming a cynical view of the world as dangerous, leaving them defenseless and powerless. Their locus of control is very external. "Why do all these bad things happen to me?" A shame-based identity is core to this behavior. Persons in the victim role have a difficult time accepting responsibility for things that happen in their lives because they either feel they are to blame (shameful/bad) or try to find someone to blame instead. This is the shame/blame cycle so frequently seen in alcoholic/incestuous families.

Issues with Touch, Body Shame and Distortions

Many people who have had boundary violations suffer from issues with touch, body shame and body distortions. Having learned that they don't deserve pleasure, touch is used instead as a method of exerting power. They have learned that touch takes away from them, is sexual or painful.

Body shame and body distortions are common responses to having been intruded upon visually and verbally and judged less than adequate. The family rules allow members to make comments and tease other members about their body. Body distortions are when individuals have confusion about their body size or shape. For instance, feelings of being very fat (when thin) or physically grotesque are responses to being scrutinized and shamed unmercifully.

Other effects of boundary violations involve having issues with spacial boundaries where persons either have no conception of personal space or require exceedingly large distances to feel safe. Boundaries are taught in the family and if members have not been taught respectful distancing techniques, they tend to wander around guessing at what is appropriate. Getting caught intruding on someone's boundaries (that they didn't even know existed) or having their own boundaries crossed are powerful shame triggers for persons with boundary problems.

Fear of Intimacy vs. Fear of Abandonment

Interpersonal relationships are filled with the potential for shame. Fears of intimacy/abandonment are conflicting needs common to people who have experienced boundary violations. The tension between these two conflicting needs/fears can cause extreme dysfunction in relationships.

Persons experiencing fear of intimacy often feel it as terror. It is a knee-jerk, instinctive response that they learned as a child. It is as if their psychic bubble has been ripped open with wide, jagged holes and they have no control over keeping themselves safe. "People who say they love me always end up hurting me." When a partner comes close, to be loving, intimate or sexual, they feel as if they have no way of protecting themselves from total enmeshment (feeling swallowed up, getting lost in the relationship). Closeness is both a signal for impending violation and the need for desperate protection. Needing something from someone or having someone need something from them is highly shame producing. Despite these danger signals, the individual remains driven towards meeting his/her intimacy needs.

Fear of abandonment operates when childhood fears conspire to maintain relationships no matter how abusive or neglectful they are. When children's closest, primary relationships were inconsistent or inadequate there often is a tendency for that child as an adult, to attempt to get all their needs met in their current relationship. Chasms in the bonding of the current relationship threaten by exposing persons to the desperate feelings of all the needs that didn't get met as children. This fear of abandonment can exert a powerful sense of desperation in relationships.

Fears of intimacy/fears of abandonment can result in the approach/avoidance common in alcoholic families. Chemicals often are used to buffer this conflict.

Shame-Based Identity

Shame severely interferes with human intimacy (Brown, Stierlin & Ravenscroft). It is developed *within* the context of interpersonal relationships and therefore so too does the pain get acted out in this arena. When the family problem-solving abilities revolve around a blame/shame cycle, no one is ever safe enough to really personally connect.

Shame Spiral

Having a shame attack is excruciating. People commonly report the experience is like having an abusive monster rise up and take over their minds. The monster replays all the terribly cruel and exposing things that they've heard over the years. The internal verbal abuse feels true. This is a set up to feel vulnerable to further exposure/abuse. When people are in a shame spiral, it can last for months. The shameful feelings tend to overpower all other feelings and can be overwhelming.

The initial response for people in a shame spiral is to turn inward, critically scrutinizing and verbally abusing themselves. Some people go totally numb in the depths of a shame spiral. Other signs to become aware of are hanging of the head, dropping of the eyes or going into a light trance (spacing out). When in a shame spiral, the immediate goal is to get safe (from people who might hurt you). People will do almost anything to not feel so badly.

One way people have learned to protect themselves from this feeling is to become rageful as a means of pushing people away (family role of scapegoat). Others become abusive (identify with the perpetrator) to feel safe. Others deny the existence of shame, putting another feeling in its place (substitution). Others try to become invisible, as being noticed increases the risk of being abused (the lost child). Others become perfectionistic, magically reasoning that if they somehow can maintain control they are safe (family hero). Others try to drink away the feelings, which for some leads to chemical dependency.

The simple concept of drinking away feelings does not take into account the special biochemical imbalances that predispose some people toward becoming chemically dependent. The diathesis stress model proposes that certain people have predispositions towards falling ill with a specific disease which they will succumb to when combined with outside stressors. Chemical dependency can be viewed in such a light. Low blood sugar syndrome, premenstrual syndrome, diabetes, vitamin deficiency, etc. have all been correlated to chemical dependency. Boundary violations, family abuse and shame are some of the stressors that can push one over the brink into addiction.

DISSOCIATION AS A SURVIVAL TOOL

One major defense mechanism utilized to protect from shame/abuse is dissociation. This is a fundamental defense mechanism and it has to take place before any other defense mechanism can operate. Dissociation is the ability to differentiate parts of our experience into segments of reality in order to process the vast amounts of information available to us. We all dissociate to some degree. A common dissociative experience is when people automatically drive cars while their minds wander (all the while unconsciously monitoring for danger).

In addition, ego state development suggests that we naturally allow parts of ourselves to specialize in certain skill areas and provide separate functions for the whole. "Personalities are divided into organized systems of behavior and experience called ego states" (Watkins & Watkins). "My business persona is different from my best friends persona which is different from how I am on the racquetball court. In each case, I am me but there are very different parts" (Hilgard's-Hidden Observer/Jung's Persona).

Dissociation and ego state development operate together as a method of defense. The ability to dissociate parts/feelings is on a continuum. One end is the driving experience. It is simply focused attention. It is a type of trance state. We all do it. Some of us are better at it than others. Some of us need it more than others.

Dissociation can be a response to shame or to any emotional trauma. A child growing up in a dysfunctional family learns very clearly which feeling/behavior are acceptable/unacceptable. In some families, the parents are like the "walking wounded," and tend to be rejecting when a child is needy because they feel so depleted themselves. The child soon learns to not *show* his/her needs but rather learns to act how the parent wants. (Winnicott's False Self/Kopp's Mask). Neediness is eventually transformed to the shadow side of the unconsciousness and the child soon learns to not *feel* need because it is a trigger for shame (Kaufman, Kopp). "The self must be denied and becomes fragmented as it fears abandonment by the parents unless it conforms" (Freed).

This experience *especially* occurs in severe forms of abuse. The ability to dissociate is in service to the ego. When the pain is bad enough, the psyche splits off from itself the experience, similar to the shock response in physical trauma. Conscious awareness is blocked and the boundaries around this experience are very rigid and nonpermeable in order to protect the self. The split off part (ego state) is encapsulated affect/memory, a disenfranchised part of the self. The affect/memory is concentrated, in its purest form (i.e., pure terror, total confusion, and/or total debased self-concept).

When dissociating, persons can block off whole parts of themselves, years of memory or whole realms of feeling experience. Some try to not feel anything. This, of course, presents problematic boundaries for persons who end up having wide gaping holes in the outside boundaries while having very rigid, nonpermeable boundaries *against themselves* on the inside. An example of this is the person on the bus who tells a perfect stranger very personal and private things while s/he is oblivious to his/her inner needs/ motives.

In extreme cases of sadistic child abuse the child can lock away whole personalities which hold the memories of abuse or who have special survival skills designed to help the child survive the horror. Multiple Personality Disorder (MPD) is when dissociation is so extreme that the ego states are fully developed into personalities. Rigid boundaries between the personalities can result in amnesia for the different parts. This is not as rare as once thought nor is it a discrete diagnosis. Increasingly, the ability to dissociate is being viewed on a continuum. (Chu, Price, Rosenthal, Ross, Watkins & Watkins) We all fit on the dissociation continuum at some point. (See Table II).

TABLE II
DISSOCIATION CONTINUUM

COMMON EXPERIENCES	HEALTHY REPRESSION	EGO STATE	MULTIPLE PERSONALITY
The driving experience.	Certain memories, feelings forgotten/ lost.	More solid configuation of separate parts.	Fully formed autonomous personalities.

People who have been shamed or abused fit further along this continuum than previously thought. Individuals can experience ego state rigidity as a defense against the pain without having a full blown Multiple Personality Disorder.

Chemical Dependency Is a Tool for Dissociation

Common defenses and family rules utilized by members in chemically dependent systems generate dissociation. Shaming parenting techniques, denial and rationalization can all impact dissociative responses. Clients who come from chemically dependent systems fit along this continuum to varying degrees.

However, full blown MPD has been observed in chemically dependent families where there was not conscious abuse or physical neglect. This would indicate that emotional boundary violations (experiencing intrusions, parental role reversals and being affectively overwhelmed) can also be important precursors to the need for dissociation (Voien & Schafer).

In addition, chemical abuse, when viewed in this light, can be seen as a tool for dissociation. It has long been recognized that some people use chemicals in order to *not* experience feelings. They use chemicals, in effect, to medicate the pain.

Interestingly enough, others use chemicals in order to access feelings previously dissociated (i.e. the woman who always gets angry when she is drunk or the woman who will allow herself to feel sexual only if she is high on marijuana). Because for women, anger and sexuality have strong social sanctions ("You should be ashamed . . .") and so therefore, many have dissociated those responses. Some need an outside agent (chemicals) to access those feelings.

Disenfranchised Parts/Encapsulated Memories

In an abusive family system, for instance, a child, in response to feeling scared and helpless in a hopeless situation, might dissociate from these feelings and start feeling very responsible and in total control. "If I clean the house and keep the other kids from fighting this afternoon then Mom won't get drunk." Little helpless feelings get delegated to the shadow side. As a coping mechanism, dissociation makes the person feel better initially but does however, preclude having any control/awareness over the experience as it is not in the unconscious.

Of course, these encapsulated memories don't just lie dormant. They still maintain an element of power. As an adult, individuals with disenfranchised feelings/encapsulated memories sometimes act out compulsively (i.e., by acting "little" like a victim to elicit someone to rescue them). The compulsion is due to the fact that these memories/feelings are beyond conscious control.

The "need" (trying to feel more safe) is helpful to the person. The "urge" (compulsion to act like a victim) was developed in response to filling this need indirectly as it wasn't safe to get it met directly. The "urge" can end up abusive and compulsive to the person, however. Other examples of this are: the need for nurturance acted out as a compulsion to overeat ("Feed me, I feel empty") or the need for safety (for an abused child) that gets acted out in withdrawal from people who care.

The "urge" seems to push the person to try again and again to get that need met/to resolve these feelings. There is a compulsive "need to repeat" the uncomfortable incident (even if they have no memory of it) so they find themselves in very familiar situations. They know what to expect, the rules of the relationship are very familiar. They do it even if they are going to inappropriate, indifferent or abusive people for need fulfillment. In fact, especially if they are going to the same types of people as their parents, the urge gets even stronger.

The "urge," if left untreated, can become addiction. This is, in part, because it has become autonomous, having been cut off from conscious awareness/control. Shame is then triggered as behavior is acted out (to fill the need) that doesn't fit the sober value system.

Other forms of compulsion seem to fit this pattern also. For instance, in families where the parents were sexually abused as children, they often find themselves turning (instead of to their partners) to their *own* children for need fulfillment. It is the author's opinion that sexual offenders who are always attracted to one particular age of children, are that age emotionally themselves. A part of them (ego state *or* MPD) is developmentally stuck at that age, desperately trying to get those needs met, albeit inappropriately. It seems to be too threatening to seek this attention in adult relationships. Some perpetrators are totally amnesic to the acting out behaviors. It is possible they go into a trance state as they act out their needs. Might not they be further along the dissociation continuum than we as counselors care to admit?

In addition, the dissociation process can be seen among clients who are physically self-abusive. Clinically, the author notes that shame seems to trigger the self-abuse when they get close to their feelings of being victimized. There are numerous reports that they feel no pain as they self-mutilate. It may be speculated that this can be due to the endorphin release caused by physical pain or their dissociative abilities or a combination of both.

This compulsion to hurt themselves can be viewed as an attempt to rectify the original abuse situation, the only way they knew how to survive their internal pain. Perhaps these abusive behaviors are what happened to them as children *or* what they wanted to do to the perpetrator (Comstock).

IMPACT OF MALE/FEMALE TRAINING ON DISSOCIATION AND CHEMICAL DEPENDENCY

In this society, there are very rigid rules about appropriate behavior for men and women. The traditional female training is to be emotional, submissive, passive, caretakers, internalizers.

This does not support women to be decisive, have achievement motivations or strength (unless they are persevering adversity). Culturally, women hold less power in this society and they learn to repress the "male" parts of themselves as unacceptable. Anger is especially discouraged and therefore disenfranchised (Isadore). Traditional female training, if taken to the extreme, can be seen as victim training. The pressures to live up to or down to one's role can be compelling and shame producing. Socialization teaches women to have shame about themselves as women. (This can also occur with racial or sexual preference minorities who, as a group, tend to internalize this cultural shame individually).

Some women turn to chemicals as a means of coping with these feelings of inadequacy. Wilsnak (1973) found that female alcoholics have chronic doubts about themselves as women (internally not fitting the stereotypical role) and so drink to feel more feminine. As they drink, their behavior, of course, does not fit the traditional female role so they feel even worse the next day. Whenever one uses chemicals to resolve feelings, it pushes the resolution further away and can lead to addiction.

Males, of course, are also not allowed many female behaviors and have learned to cut off the parts of themselves that do not fit the traditional male role. Traditional male training is to be decisive, unemotional, externalizers, achievement and action oriented. Sexually, men are taught to always want sex, as their masculinity depends on "scoring." Male training, taken to the extreme, can be seen as victimizer training. The assumption of a rigid definition of traditional sex roles by either or both partners can cause problems within relationships.

With the socialization process teaching each sex to disenfranchise major parts of themselves, there is a tendency for "half people" to wander around desperately trying to find other "half people" to make themselves whole. When "one meets ones match" (the traditional roles fit like puzzle pieces) it is like ripping oneself in half to think about breaking up the relationship. This, in part, addresses why it is so hard to break addictive relationships.

When men and women break the traditional rules of their socialized behavior, there is often a shame response. Sterne, Schaefer and Evans (1983) reported that among their sample of

75 chemically dependent women, 13% admitted to sexually abusing a minor. Breaking the cultural role of nurturer/mother becomes unbearable for some clients to admit. The shame for this is immense and the quality of their sobriety is threatened. Without acknowledging and working through this issue, the likelihood of their relapse is high.

On the other hand, many men are now admitting that they were sexually abused as children also. Their male training disallowed them to see this as abuse as they were supposed to always want/be ready for sex. To be trained-in sexually by an older person is, for some, a male cultural ideal. The reality is that this is child abuse.

Just as we as professionals have had to learn to ask women about being victims of abuse, we now need to ask the questions about female perpetration and male victimization. This can be an extreme shame trigger for clients. We need to ask with compassion and sensitivity to timing as some people in recovery need a period of sobriety before opening up these issues while others couldn't maintain any period of recovery without addressing these issues immediately in treatment.

THERAPEUTIC RECOVERY MODELS

Time limited therapy such as chemical dependency treatment programs can have a major impact on the education, assessment and gentle openings of these issues. Shame, boundary work and reclaiming dissociated parts can all be begun in chemical dependency treatment but full resolution most frequently requires long-term therapy.

Boundary Work

The counseling relationship has the potential to be, for some people, the first significant relationship that is respectful of their boundaries. The best way for professionals to teach clients about boundaries is to have clear boundaries themselves. (See Nielsen article.)

Typically in traditional chemical dependency treatment the approach has been to break down denial and cause clients to feel distrustful of themselves and overpowered by their compulsions. Old style heavy confrontations (hot seat techniques) are intrusive and harmful to people who have had their boundaries previously violated.

It is especially crucial for chemically dependent women who have had high rates of abuse to not be further violated. People who have been victimized know exactly how to deal with intrusive therapeutic confrontations because they have survived much more severe forms of it. They either become compliant (passively acting in the way they think you want them to act) or defiant (possibly the only way they know how to maintain any semblance of their own identity).

Providing an environment that is supportive and nonshaming enough to allow clients to drop their defenses rather than blasting away at them is a much more helpful technique (Evans & Schaefer). When needed, loving, gentle confrontation, is much more productive and respectful. Chemically dependent women especially need to be able to feel and claim their power back (or maybe claim it for the first time).

Boundary work for clients needs to be addressed internally and externally. External boundary work involves teaching the client new behavioral skills such as assertiveness training, stopping the compulsive/self-defeating behaviors and beginning self-care behaviors. Internal boundary work is encouraging the client toward self-definition (suggest s/he make judgements such as "I like, I don't like" a hundred times a day to help define their preferences), decision-making (allow even in the counseling relationship to encourage client ownership of the therapy), and imaging work (visualization of new boundaries, ego strengthening exercises and fantasizing new assertive behaviors).

Shame Recovery Model

As professionals, it is crucial to never actively shame clients. This is intrusive and a repeat of the family environment. If we *do* shame clients, we become one of the abusers, untrustable. It is, however, important to not tiptoe around clients' shame as it can cover issues that need to be addressed. Some people have learned to use shame as a defense. A shame spiral is so excruciating that professionals can share the client's tendency to try to avoid triggering it. As professionals, it is helpful to bring clients right up to their shame gently and support them through the experience. This is very painful and many clients doubt they can survive such intense pain. This is when clients' survival techniques are brought out for protection. It is a high risk time for self-abusive or destructive behaviors. We as professionals need to be able to witness their shame and still be consistently there for them.

Gently supporting individuals in a shame spiral to lift up their eyes in order to make human contact slows the shame spiral. Suggesting that they get reality checks from people close to them to check out how they are viewed might also help.

Finally, it is helpful to educate the client about the steps out of a shame spiral: relationship, recognition, stopping the inner abuse and affirming the self.

1st Step – Relationship. The main element in healing a shame-based identity is in developing a caring relationship with someone trustable. This is what Kaufman calls "reconnecting the interpersonal bridge." A therapeutic relationship is exceedingly important in that the counselor has an immense amount of power (to nurture or abuse). It is important that trust be maintained and guarded by both parties. Within this relationship it is helpful to explore where the person learned to feel shame. Who shamed them? What did they get shamed for? How did they deal with it? What effect does it have on them now? What is their favorite way of protecting themselves from the feelings?

2nd Step – Recognition. This process needs to be accomplished in stages. At first it is quite enough simply to be able to recognize and label the shame experience. This can be difficult as the shame ego state can be very elusive. At this stage the defenses should slowly drop (out of trust and safety rather than by counselor confrontation). This is a difficult time for clients because they come to experience the full blown intensity of their shame. This is the part in therapy where it gets worse before it gets better. Predict this and also project an image of hope.

3rd Step – Stopping the inner abuse. Stopping the tapes that replay abusive messages is a crucial but difficult step. It is a compulsive response with attending physical behaviors so it is important to monitor the other ways they get abusive too. Teach thought-stopping techniques in order to interrupt the negative cognitions. Work on a behavioral level by teaching them to stop being mean to themselves (literally hundreds of times a day). It is helpful to have a cue sentence that helps them attend to this process. "This is shame, this is what it felt like growing up in my family. I'm not going to listen to the abuse anymore because it's only lies."

4th Step—Affirming the self. Teach self-affirmations. This is important in order to neutralize the toxic wastes. Talk through, draw pictures, make a collage etc. of their shame. Help them to visualize it, what part of the body is it stored, color of it, etc. Slowly move it out of the body and bury it in the ground. Visualize the body fresh and clean.

Occasionally, clients find it difficult to release the shame response even with hard therapeutic work. It has been helpful to consider how this shame response has been functional. In some cases, it was discovered that feeling the total awfulness of shame was less painful than some other trauma. In some the feeling was total helplessness/hopelessness/terror. They would rather take the full blame ("feel shame, I'm bad, it's all my fault") because it had some power in it rather than feel how little and helpless they were in a totally crazy situation. Sometimes keeping the shame identity feels like the lessor of two evils.

Healing Dissociation

Making Friends with the Junkie is an important step in the healing process. It involves helping clients come to the understanding that their compulsions are parts of themselves, not some shameful, sick thing to be hidden. Feeling a need to drink or acting out in "Junkie" or dry drunk behavior can be interpreted as a sign to attend to their needs. Learning and accepting compulsive feelings as an indicator that they need to take care of themselves more carefully can be an important learning tool. Appropriate referral to long-term therapy such as individual therapy or group work can address these recovery needs more fully.

Ego State Therapy

Ego state therapy is a longer term therapeutic approach utilized to reduce conflicts between conflicting ego states that constitute a family (in an individual). It involves providing group or family therapy within the person. Its goal is to help clients reclaim the totality of themselves, the various disenfranchised parts, the experiences, memories, feelings, and reality of what it was like to survive an impossible situation being so little (Watkins & Watkins).

Each ego state, no matter how dysfunctional/abusive now, was created to help the person survive. It is therapeutically important not to try to eliminate/fuse the ego states because this will elicit great resistance. It would be as dangerous to the therapeutic relationship as if we were conducting therapy with a family and we told the 16-year-old that she was the problem child and needed to leave. Don't eliminate parts, just make boundaries between the parts more permeable.

The goal of therapy is to try to meet the needs of all ego states in a constructive way to ease the conflicts. It is also imperative to help clients stop the self-abusive/defeating behaviors and to begin to become self-nurturing. In that the child-within has experienced a great deal of neglect/abuse, a therapist or spouse can't substitute for the child-need for nurturance. It is important to support a mothering part of the person themselves to nurture the child-within.

Drawing pictures and writing letters to the various parts of the self is a helpful way to explore the separateness. Doing visualization exercises or using hypnosis (if the professional is trained in these skills) are exceptionally powerful tools towards integration of the disenfranchised parts.

CONCLUSION

This article has attempted to draw together various understandings about how shame impacts individuals growing up in chemically dependent families. It discusses the concepts of boundary formation, boundary violations and the resulting consequences to identity as it relates to shame dynamics in families. It further develops the idea of dissociation as a functional reaction to shame and other boundary violations. The article concludes with a discussion of therapeutic techniques for addressing these issues.

REFERENCES

Brown, J., Shame, Intimacy and Sexuality. *Alcoholism Treatment Quarterly*. In Press.

Chodrow, N., (1974). Family Structures and Feminine Personality. In *Women, Culture and Society*. (Ed.) Michelle Simbalist Rosaldo & Louise Lamphere. California: Stanford University Press.

Chu, J., (1985). *Dissociation Continuum: Towards a Rational Diagnosis of Multiple Personality and Dissociative Disorders*. The Second International Conference on Multiple Personality and Dissociative States.

Coleman, E., (1986). Chemical Dependency and Intimacy Dysfunction: Inextricably Bound. *Journal of Chemical Dependency Treatment, 1*.

Coleman, E. & Colgan, P., Boundary Inadequacy in Chemically Dependent Families. *Journal of Psychoactive Drugs*. In Press.

Comstock, C., (1986). *The Therapeutic Utilization of Abreactive Experiences in the Treatment of Multiple Personality Disorder*. The Third International Conference on Multiple Personality and Dissociative States.

Ellis, G., (1986). Pathfinder Program. Adolescent Treatment Goals. Mounds Park Hospital.

Erickson, E., (1963). *Childhood and Society*. New York: Norton.

Evans, S., (1986). Shame. *Manual for the Model Women's Treatment Project*. State of Minnesota.

Evans, S., & Schaefer, S., Incest and Chemically Dependent Women: Treatment Considerations. *Journal of Chemical Dependency Treatment*. In Press.

Freed, A., (1984). Differentiating Between Borderline and Narcissistic Personalities. *Social Casework: The Journal of Contemporary Social Work*.

Hammer, S., (1976). *Mothers and Daughters/Daughters and Mothers*. New York: Signet Books.

Hilgard, E., (1977). *Divided Consciousness: Multiple Controls in Human Thought and Action*. New York: John Wiley and Sons.

Isadore, S., (1986). *The Role and Function of Dissociative Reactions in Society*. Proceedings of the Third International Conference on Multiple Personality and Dissociative States.

Jung, C., (1971). (ed.) Joseph Campbell, New York: The Viking Press.

Kaplan, L., (1978). *Oneness and Separateness: From Infant to Individual*. New York: Simon Schuster.

Kaufman, G., (1974). The Meaning of Shame: Toward a Self-Affirming Identity. *Journal of Counseling Psychology, 21*.

Kaufman, G., (1974). *On Shame, Identity and Dynamics of Change*. Paper presented at the American Psychological Association, New Orleans.

Kaufman, G., (1980). *Shame, the Power of Caring*. Cambridge: Shenkman.

Kaufman, G. & Raphael, L., (1982). *Relating to the Self: Changing Inner Dialogue*. Paper presented at the American Psychological Association, Washington D.C.

Klein, M., (1948). *Theory of Anxiety and Guilt*. New York: Delacort Press.

Kopp, S., (1980). *Mirror, Mask and Shadow: The Risks and Rewards of Self Acceptance*. New York: MacMillan.

Mahler, M., (1972). A Study of the Separation/Individuation Process and Its Possible Application to Borderline Phenomena in the Psychoanalytic Situation. *In The Psychoanalytic Study of the Child*. Vol. 26., New York: Quadrangel Books.

May, R., (1972). *Power and Innocence: A Search for the Source of Violence*. Dell Publishers.

Miller, A., (1981). *The Drama of the Gifted Child: How Narcissistic Parents Form and Deform the Emotional Lives of Their Children*. New York: Basic Books.

Neilsen, L., (1984). Sexual Abuse and Chemical Dependency: Assessing the Risk for Women Alcoholics and Adult Children. *Focus on Family*, Nov./Dec. Issue.

Price, R., (1986). *Dissociative Disorders of the Self: A Continuum Extending into Multiple Personality*. The Third International Conference on Multiple Personality and Dissociative States.

Rosenthal, R., (1985). *The Diagnosis of Partial Forms of Multiple Personality Disorder*. The Second International Conference on Multiple Personality and Dissociative States.

Ross, C., (1984). *DSM III: Problems in Diagnosing Partial Forms of Multiple Personality Disorder*. The First International Conference on Multiple Personality and Dissociative States.

Schaefer, S. & Evans, S., Women's Sexuality and the Process of Recovery. *Journal of Chemical Dependency Treatment*. In Press.

Sterne, M., Schaefer, S. & Evans, S., (1983). Women's Sexuality and Alcoholism. *Alcoholism-Analysis of a World Wide Problem*. Lancaster, England: MTP Press.

Stierline, H. & Ravenscroft, K., (1972). Varieties of Adolescent Separation Conflicts. *British Journal of Medical Psychiatry, 45*.

Voien, B, & Schafer, D., (1986). *MPD: Alcoholism and Unconscious Abuse—The Traumatizing Environment*. The Third International Conference on Multiple Personality and Dissociative Disorders.

Watkins, J., (1978). *The Therapeutic Self*. New York: Human Sciences Press.

Watkins, H. & Watkins, J., (1979-80). Ego States and Hidden Observers. *Journal of Altered States of Consciousness. 5.*

Watkins, H. & Walkins, J., (1984). *Hypnosis Conference*. Stillwater, MN.

Watkins, H., (1984). Ego-State Theory and Therapy. In *Encyclopedia of Psychology*. (Ed.) R. J. Corsini, New York: Wiley, Vol. 1.

Watkins, J. & Watkins, H., (1984). Hazards to the Therapist in the Treatment of Multiple Personalities. *Psychiatric Clinics of North America*. Vol. 7, No. 1.

Wilsnack, S., (1973). Sex Role Identity in the Female Alcoholic. *The Journal of Abnormal Psychology*. Vol. 82.

Winnicott, D., (1965). *The Maturational Process and Pathological Narcissism*. London: Hogarth Press.

Shame and Forgiving in Alcoholism

Beverly J. Flanigan, MSSW

SUMMARY. The difficulty in healing shame is that there is no interpersonal process to relieve it, as contrasted with guilt. The author describes the forgiving process which restores relationships. Clinicians are given guidelines to help their clients foster the process of forgiving in alcoholic families.

I sometimes think that shame, mere awkward, senseless shame, does much more towards preventing good acts and straightforward happiness as any of our vices can do.

C. S. Lewis
A Grief Observed

INTRODUCTION

The problem with shame is there is no quick or prescribed way out of it. It is not as though a person in shame, fleeing from raging flames of accusation, can simply take the nearest fire escape to safety. Instead, the escape from shame is more like an escape from Houdini's black box. Observers on the shore who watch as the shackled box is lowered into the water believe that there must be some methodical process by which Houdini releases himself from the seemingly impossible tangle of chains and locks. Otherwise he would not take such a risk. Yet when the magician bobs out of the water as though he's been serenely observing the fish life below, those observers still feel that a mysti-

---

Beverly J. Flanigan is Clinical Associate Professor, Department of Social Work, University of Wisconsin at Madison.

181

cal, inexplicable metamorphosis of some kind has occurred. No human, no matter how flexible, could have found his way out of the box and to the surface. It is this way with shame. We do not know how people escape it or heal from its wounds; and, if some people *do* escape, we might tend to attribute it to something magical or to deny that it was shame to begin with.

This paper will explore the escape from and metamorphosis of shame. It will focus on some of the psychological twists and turns a shamed person goes through in order to be freed from this debilitating affect. Particularly it will explore the relationship between shame, guilt, and forgiving, with forgiving being viewed as the first breath of air felt in the shamed person's lungs after being held under water for too long. Finally, it will tie together shame and forgiving in families where alcoholism exists.

THE DIFFICULTY OF SHAME

Why is shame so difficult? A quote from Herbert Morris might begin to shed light on this question. "One cannot be forgiven one's shame and punishment does not divest one of it" (Morris, 62).

Morris goes on to say that there can be no amends made for shame, that there can be no apologies made for one's shame. In other words, there is no *interpersonal process for being relieved of one's shame*. Shame is an isolating affect (Aristotle, 109; Gaylin, 54-74). It is a failure by comparison, not commission. Shame results from falling short on some scale where a person fails to do the extraordinary. It does not result from a failure to comply with reasonable demands (Morris, 59-63). The language of amending and forgiving then is not only not applicable to shame, it is not appropriate.

It would be inappropriate, for example, to ask forgiveness for being "too short," just as it would be inappropriate to ask forgiveness for being "too naive," or "too unable to help," or "too" anything. Shame results from a failure of heroics or a failure to be more like someone else; or it simply results from our being ourselves and not someone else. There can be no appropriate amends or apologies for being who we are. Nor should there be. If a person puts himself[1] in a position of hearing apologies or "forgiving" someone for merely being *who he is* (i.e., not what he has *done*), then that person has placed himself on a higher moral plane than other people. This is inappropriate. For shame, then, there is no good amends or apologies, there is no interpersonal mechanism by which it is removed, and there can be no forgiveness of it. There are, however, mechanisms for amending guilt.

AMENDING GUILT

Guilt, as a feeling state, (not a legal determination) stems from violating a moral rule (Lampert, Downie, Kurtz, Martin). Like shame, it is an affect associated with self-disliking and remorse (Gaylin). There are differences between guilt and shame however, especially in the recovery from guilt. Guilt's recovery is more like taking the nearest fire exit to safety below.

Where there is guilt, there are distinct and identifiable "agents" involved, and four processes of remediation, all of which have some order to them. Both the agents and the processes of remediation deserve some attention. Guilt has two agents — the guilty *offender* and the one who has been *offended*, or harmed, by the violation of some moral rule (Martin).

The guilty offender is one who breaks a moral rule between himself and another person and who feels guilty for it. The offended person is one who shared this rule, believed in its worth, and was harmed by its violation. An offended person might be an intimate associate of the offender or someone he does not know.[2] More often than not though, when a person commits an offense that makes him feel guilty, the person he has harmed is someone he knows well.

A guilty person, then, is one who perceives himself to have transgressed or to have violated some moral rule or law. He is the "offender." He also sees himself as (1) responsible or account-

---

[1] "He," "him," "himself" and "his" are to be gender-free pronouns used to refer to women and men.

[2] An example where the offended person is unknown might be a hotel maid who is harmed when an offender steals a towel and it is the maid who will be forced to pay for it.

able (2) morally negligent or reprehensible and (3) needing to make repairs (Martin). For example, a woman who feels guilty for taking money from her friend's purse first must believe that she violated not only a law, but also an implicit agreement between friends. To feel guilty, she must also feel (1) that she has caused an offense (i.e., is accountable), (2) that she was wrong in doing it, and (3) that she must seek out her friend to apologize to her and to try to mend their friendship.

The other agent in guilt, the "offended" can then do one of several things in response to the offender. She can refuse to see the person again and terminate their relationship or she can begin a process through which the two engage in some form of interpersonal interaction. It is through this interaction that the guilt will be dealt with in one way or another.

It is commonly thought that there are four interpersonal processes associated with an offense where guilt exists. These processes are (1) pardoning, (2) condoning, (3) punishing and (4) forgiving (Downie, 132; Martin). Some distinctions are necessary.

Pardoning usually refers to an act of proclamation by an authority (a governor, for example) whereby a guilty person is not required to be held up to punishment or to make restitution for his offense (Lampert, 13). Condoning simply means to overlook as though no harm has come of one's offense or there was no harm intended. A wife, for example, might condone her husband's flirtation because he was drunk and therefore, she feels he did not intend to do harm. These two reactions, pardoning and condoning, result in letting the guilty party "off the hook" so to speak. The guilt should end there.

The other two responses, punishment and forgiving are much more involved processes. They involve not only *not* condoning a violation of a rule, but rather they insist that the broken rule be held up for reexamination and reassessment.

Punishment serves to remind an offender that some specific rule has been broken (Morris 103-108; Martin). In punishing someone, the punisher asks himself "will this punishment make it clear that a rule was broken and that this infraction cannot be taken lightly?" If someone is retaliating, on the other hand, he asks himself "will causing this person to suffer make me feel better?" (Martin). The goal of retaliation is self-gratification. It is not important what happens to a relationship as a result. The goal of punishment is to remind both the offender and the offended what rules they think should guide their relationship. Punishment is a stepping-stone to reaffirming those rules, and to the final reaffirmation of the relationship itself—forgiving.

Forgiving, the fourth option available to the offended, both reminds the offender of the specific rule that was broken and results in reviewing that rule (Flanigan, Martin). It also results in reaccepting the offender as a person of moral worth—a good person (Lampert). It is forgiving which is the most complete and repairing of the four options, and it is through forgiveness that equality and equilibrium are restored to the relationship between the guilty offender and the person he has hurt.

Imagine a teenager to have stayed out past curfew. His parents might admonish him first, remind him of the rule of the house second, and ground him for a month, third. The punishment acts to refresh the violator's memory as to the rules of the house. If the parent also in his heart reaccepts the wayward teen, he also forgives him.

Forgiving is an outcome of a process where one person, a guilty party, has offended or wounded another, where the wound or offense is identified and examined; and where there has been blame attributed to one party for having offended the other (that is, where there is a clear offender and offended person). It is also a process which includes punishment (real or imagined), a decision to repair the relationship, and a reaffirmation of the goodness of a rule which has been broken and the person who broke it (Flanigan). If we were to view forgiving as an interpersonal process between two people, it might look as depicted in Figure 1.

In function, forgiving ends one relational state and begins another (Flanigan). It restores peace to a relationship, clarifies the rules which will govern people's behaviors towards each other, and reaffirms the moral integrity of both the rules and the parties involved in upholding them. It is a healing process which restores equilibrium in interpersonal relationships. Of course, the process can break down at any point, but once completed, people

Figure 1:   The Interaction of Forgiving

The Offender:		The Offended:	
(1)	Violates a known rule	(1)	Names the moral rule that was broken
(2)	Feels guilt, remorse, self-disgust	(2)	Feels betrayed, angry
(3)	Apologizes	(3)	Blames the offender
(4)	Offender held "at bay"; not allowed back into the relationship	(4)	Tells the offender the degree of damage done to self and to relationship
(5)	Promises to not repeat the rule violation	(5)	Punishes the offender (either actually or figuratively)
(6)	Promises to reaccept the rule as it has been stated	(6)	Reassesses the appropriateness of the moral rule and decides whether to restore it as a governing ideal in the relationship
(7)	Believes the offended person holds him to be worthy again	(7)	Agrees to restore the rule to the relationship and decides to accept the offender's promises and him as a person of integrity

are able to move on and put old grievances behind them (Flanigan, Lampert, 63-64).

Offenses or injuries caused by rule violation, then, evoke, on the part of the guilty person, feelings of contrition, responsibility, moral negligence, and needs to make repairs. The injured or offended person can respond by pardoning, condoning, punishing, or forgiving the offender. Even where the offended person is not available, the guilty person can (1) admit the rule he violated to someone else; (2) blame himself; (3) promise himself to not violate the rule again; (4) make restitution; and (5) reestablish the rule as a guideline for his life. In other words, he can pardon, punish, and even forgive himself. Even if self-pardoning is less healing than self-forgiving, it "resets the clock" and allows a person to begin anew.

It is forgiving which the guilty seek, and, as we shall see later, it is forgiving which the ashamed also seek.

SHAME

Where there is shame there has been no violation of a rule, that is no actual offense committed (Gaylin, Kurtz, Morris). Yet, the ashamed person feels very deeply that he has offended someone through his falling short and his inability to be something he is not.

The ashamed person holds very similar feelings to the guilty person. He feels (1) responsible and accountable for having done something wrong, and he feels (2) morally negligent or reprehensible. He probably also shares with the guilty a sense of contrition and self-disgust (Gaylin). What he does not share with the guilty is a sense of a clear rule violation. Nor does he share with the guilty the capacity to recognize who it is he has offended. Nor can he clearly blame anyone for an infraction of a rule. In other words, he cannot attribute blame to anyone for *doing* anything. He is not sure what he is guilty of.

The person in shame does not share with the guilty an orderly process of repair for his ruptured relationships with others. Shame does not rupture relationships. An ashamed person may end a relationship because of his shame, but shame itself does not end it. And the ashamed person cannot, for all his shame, engage in an interpersonal process to expunge it. That is, shame cannot be pardoned, condoned, punished, or forgiven. What can he do then to escape from shame? A beginning answer will emerge from understanding the agents involved in shame.

In guilt, there are two agents: The offender and the offended. In shame there is only one active agent — the offender. There are two other "silent partners" in shame, however; and it is these silent partners who play a major role in the transformation of shame.

When a person falls prey to shame, he feels deeply that he has not behaved in a way or taken some heroic action that another, better person, might have taken. We are labeling this "better" person "the comparison person." This ideal person could be a sibling, friend, Rambo, Eleanor Roosevelt, or even Buddha. Regardless, the comparison person is the person being held up as the yardstick for comparison because the comparison person, it is thought, need never be ashamed of his actions. His actions are proper and good. This "comparison person" in the mind of the ashamed would have handled the situation which evoked shame differently. He represents both the ideal good and all that the ashamed person is not. He is the person the ashamed person never could be.

The second agent in shame is the "imaginary offended person." This person is the one perceived to be the victim of the ashamed person's frailties and the recipient of his falling short. It is this person, in the mind of the ashamed, who suffers because of his weaknesses. For example, a child might think he wounded or offended his mother because he got into a fight on the playground. (It was actually the other child who was wounded!) But the child perceives his mother to be offended because she thought he was "above brutality."

An attribute of the "imaginary offended person" is that he is not necessarily aware that he holds that position. He may not be present; or he may be a person in the offender's past, perhaps a parent figure. Regardless, it is this person, in the mind of the offender, who is in a position to judge him as flawed.

The third agent in shame is the person who feels ashamed – the offender. This is actually a "perceived offender" just as the other two roles are perceived but not necessarily valid. Again, the ashamed person believes that his very being is offensive and that through failing to be extraordinary he has let someone down or injured someone and his relationship with him.

What are the ways taken out of shame? In chapter one four responses to shame are mentioned, these being rage, grandiosity, perfectionism, and withdrawal. There may, however, be another very important route the shamed person, in his Houdini's box, goes through to find his way to air. He may put himself in a position in which he balances off his shame with goodness so that his frailties are condoned. Or he may convert his shame to guilt. The purpose of the conversion of shame to guilt is this: shame has no mechanism for repair. There is no way shame can be removed or erased or made right. There is no way to end shame and start over; and there is no interpersonal means for healing it. For guilt there are all of these options.

While shame may become a "core" affect for some (Kaufman), it is also assumed here that an organism will seek a state of equilibrium when and if it is out of balance (Piaget, 840). It is a contention here that shame will cause disequilibrium, and when it does, it will transform itself like any other transient feeling (happiness, fear, anger, love). Shame does not simply pile up on itself like so many bricks in a stack.

It is also thought that shame will transform itself in a way that (1) it can be expressed in some fashion to another person and (2) it can lend itself to a process through which it is remediated or removed. At the very least, the feeling of shame acts as a trigger to one's cognitive processes, or to "the thinking brain," that tells the person in shame that he should "do something about it" (Gaylin p. 6-8).

Figure 2 indicates that in all cases of shame, the ashamed person can find no rule he has broken and yet that he feels contrite, responsible, and morally reprehensible (columns 1 and 2). Column 3 indicates that the ashamed person can or cannot identify any known "comparison person" (e.g., a parent, friend, or T.V. hero) to whom he has fallen short. Column 4 indicates that the ashamed person can or cannot identify a specific person he has offended. Column 5 indicates the array of possible behaviors displayed by the ashamed person under three different circumstances (i.e., set 1, set 2, or set 3). Column 6 identifies the function of adopting these different behaviors as shame transforms itself (to transform itself to something which can be condoned, punished, or forgiven).

In set 1 the ashamed person has fallen short by comparison to some known person (Perhaps a friend or even a religious figure). Here the offender might try to be more like this particular "comparison person" through imitating him or trying to be perfect or above moral judgment. The function of this behavior is to balance off the shame with goodness so no other shortcomings go unnoticed or are condoned. (So what if he drinks once in a while, look how much he has done for his community.)

A clinical example is a female recovering client (also a COA) who tried desperately to emulate Jackie Onassis. Jackie, even in extreme pain responded with dignity, propriety, and grace (unlike the client). The client felt that if she could be more like Jackie, perhaps her other faults would be less noticeable and her life, as a result, less painful.

Figure 2

THE TRANSFORMATION OF SHAME

SET	FEELING STATE	COMPARISON PERSON	IMAGINARY OFFENDED PERSON	OUTCOME BEHAVRIOR	FUNCTION
SET 1	contrition	known	not known	1. attempting to be like comparison person	to offset shame with excellence or perfection
	falling short			2. imitating "the hero"	to have other frailties condoned or overlooked
	morally reprehensible			3. attempting to be perfect	
				4. admonishing others for their shortcomings	
SET 2	self-loathing	not known	known	1. apologizing continually	to begin process of punishment or forgiving by identifying rule violated & getting offended person to place blame on the offender
	no good			2. inquiring, what, if anything, has been done wrong	
				3. seeking affirmation of approval from offended person	
				4. confessing where no rule has been broken	
SET 3		not known	not known	1. withdrawing	to begin process of forgiving through becoming guilty or identifying how one has failed or broken some known rule
				2. acting out, breaking rules	
				3. seeking affirmation from many sources	
				4. seeking approval	
				5. violating normal standards	
				6. accepting punishment where there are no violations	

In set 2, the ashamed person thinks that he has let a specific person down, but he does not know in relation to what "comparison person." The outcome behaviors indicated in Figure 2 are continual apologizing, inquiring whether something is wrong, seeking approval or affirmation, and confessing where there is nothing to confess. The function of these behaviors is to get the offended person to identify a rule which has been broken, or a comparison person to emulate, or to attribute blame to him so that he can be forgiven.

A clinical example here might be the child of an alcoholic father who constantly asks her mother (who always seems disappointed in her) if she is pretty, or if her grades are good enough, or if she should try to be more like her aunt. If the mother finally gets angry because of her daughter's bothersome questions, the daughter can be reprimanded for violating a rule and "pushing her mother too far." Then the daughter can apologize, ask forgiveness, and promise to not bother her mother again.

In set 3, the ashamed person does not know by what standard he has fallen short, or whom he has offended or what rules he has broken. Here we may see a transformation of shame which manifests in frequent rule violations, frequently taking opportunities to be blamed, and frequent approval—seeking from a variety of sources. This ashamed person is on a "fishing expedition"— fishing for rules, "comparison people" against whom he might judge himself, and methods of offending people so that clear rules between the offender and offended can be established and some process of remediation begun.

These behaviors might manifest clinically in a client's not showing up for appointment, not completing outside assignments and so forth. By breaking agreements he can get the clinician to restate rules, perhaps to punish him, and finally to reaccept him as a person of moral worth.

SHAME TRANSFORMATION IN ALCOHOLISM

How does this shame transformation work where there is alcoholism, and what can a clinician do in response to it?

First let's go back to two known sources of shame for both the alcoholic and those who love him. The first source of shame is that no one has been able to prevent the alcoholism or stop it from taking its course. All heroics have failed on the part of both the alcoholic and his family members. The illness itself is a source of shame because something is wrong with someone; not with what he does, but what he is (Becker, Kurtz). So in alcoholism, something is wrong with someone and no amount of heroics, or love, or intervention can help him. Everyone falls short. This is the first source of shame. The second is that everyone has endured the humiliation of alcoholism. They all, both the alcoholic and his family, just stood there and "took it," revealing themselves to be weak and ineffectual in the eyes of their families, their friends, and their community. They looked like willing "gluttons-for-punishment" to the outside world, who knew nothing of their strengths. As one recovering client said, as he broke down crying when talking about his own alcoholic father's physical abuse of him: "I had to just stay there and take it. If I hadn't, I'd have killed the son-of-a-bitch." This man chose shame over guilt.

Other sources of shame stem from the well-known inconsistencies in an alcoholic family (Ablon, Downs). Not only are rules broken repeatedly so that guilt abounds, but more often than not, no one is sure what the family rules are. Family members may develop their sense of right and wrong in a hit-and-miss fashion. Of course, this is a perfect place for shame to germinate since no one knows what the proper behavior is and against what standard he falls short if he fails. He just repeatedly fails for some reason unknown to himself. In addition, in an alcoholic family it is often impossible to find a comparison person as a standard by which to measure oneself. Everyone may seem so frail, faulty, and inconsistent, or so powerful, controlling, and mean.

The sources of shame in alcoholic families, then, are numerous. But three given sources are (1) the alcoholism itself (2) the humiliation felt by those who just stayed and "lived with it" and who "left it" and (3) the inconsistent, often incompatible rules which abound in the alcoholic family. In addition, there may be no available standards of comparison in the family itself.

Applying the transformation of shame model to alcoholism, then, we might see this: In set 1, where the person tries to absolve shame by rising to a place beyond disapproval, we may see alcoholics becoming more like their sponsors or becoming alcoholism professionals. We might see family members becoming helpers like those who attempted to help their families and who, at the time, seemed above reproach.

If these seemingly well people find themselves in need of help, clinicians might first recognize that these clients still do not know how they failed or whom they failed. Nothing has been repaired; instead they have become people who are "not shameful" (Morris, 62). This may be enough. However, if this is not enough these people may bring to a clinician a beginning recognition that the balancing act between perfection and shame is resulting still in the see-saw sliding toward shame; and they might feel acutely the need to look for mechanisms for remedying shame and finding forgiveness for it.

In set 2, the ashamed person is seeking to know by what standard he failed. In alcoholic families the child may see himself as not being enough like the perfect child next door. The spouse might think she should have endured longer and been more patient. She is "too impatient" or "too soft" or "too controlling." She may bring to the clinician a litany of apologies and attempts to get affirmation. Neither will undo her shame.

A clinical picture here might be a child of an alcoholic or a spouse who brings to a therapist apologies, lists of recent wrong-doings, confessions of imagined wrong-doings or attempts at approval. Unwittingly, the therapist might engage in approval-giving, when the client actually needs to sort through why she feels disapproved of in the first place.

In set 3, the alcoholic or his family members might act out, run away, get drunk, have affairs, or any number of things to violate some known rule. Much like the behavior in set 2, these behaviors are designed to make rules real, to be able to feel contrite for something tangible, to be able to apologize for something one did (not something he is), and to be able to be forgiven.

FORGIVING AND ALCOHOLISM

Forgiving again, lets someone back into the human fold. It is the process through which one rejoins the human race after having been cast aside. Forgiving is the one mechanism through which amends can be made, apologies can be given and received, blame can be cast, punishment delivered and restoration of the moral worth of the person and the rightness of interpersonal rules reaffirmed (Flanigan).

How can a clinician foster a process of forgiving in an alcoholic family? First he can recognize the client's behavior as an attempt to restore his equilibrium, through balancing off his shame with something more positive. Secondly, he can recognize some specific behavior as possible manifestations of the transformation of shame (Figure 2).

Thirdly, the clinician can begin the process of forgiving — either helping the client to forgive himself or helping him to forgive another person (Figure 1). This means the clinician will begin to help the client find moral rules, attribute blame, understand who offended whom, search for appropriate punishments, decide whether to develop or reinstate certain rules as guidelines for conducting his life, and decide whether to accord the offender, whoever he is, a place of dignity and worth in the client's life (Flanigan).

Beginning questions for the practitioner to ask himself are these: (1) What moral rules were broken? (2) Who broke them? (3) Who wrote them? (4) Who should be blamed? (5) What are the rules now? (6) How has punishment happened? (7) Who is responsible for rewriting the moral rules if the client does not think they are fair? (8) Who are comparison people? (9) Do they represent the moral law? (10) Can the client decide that he is responsible for letting himself or another "off the hook?"

These are only beginning questions, but should serve as basic guidelines for helping the practitioner to identify the role he needs to play in the forgiving process and the extent to which the process must occur.

CONCLUSION

The ashamed person trapped in his "Houdini's box" struggles alone under the water twisting and turning to come to the surface, hear the applause of his friends, and rejoin the people on the shore.

The perceptive Alcohol and Other Drug Abuse clinician will recognize some of the twists and turns as attempts to transform shame into something that can be amended; and, in his sensitivity, the compassionate professional will undertake steps to promote an interpersonal process which has, to now, been associated with amending guilt, that is, pardoning, condoning, punishing, or forgiving. Forgiving, the most healing of these, will allow the client to finally put a painful, entrapped, and maladaptive part of his life behind him, leave the shackled box below in the water, and come up for air.

REFERENCES

Ablon, Joan, "Family Structure and Behavior in Alcoholism: A Review of the Literature," in B. Kissin & H. Begleiter (eds.), *The Biology of Alcoholism IV. Social Aspects of Alcoholism*, NY: Plenum, 1976.

Aristotle, *Nichomachean Ethics*, Indianapolis: The Liberal Arts Press, 1962.

Becher, Ernest, *Escape from Evil*, NY: The Free Press, 1975.

Downie, R. S., "Forgiveness," *The Philosophical Quarterly*, 15, 128-134, 1965 (April).

Downs, William R., "Alcoholism as a Developing Family Crisis," *Family Relations*, 31, 5-12, 1982 (January).

Flanigan, Beverly, *Forgiving the Unforgivable*, Book manuscript in progress.

Gaylin, Willard, *Feelings*, NY: Ballantine, 1979.

Kaufman, Gershen, *Shame: The Power of Caring*, Cambridge, MA: Schenkman, 1980.

Kurtz, Ernest, "Why AA Works," *Journal of Studies on Alcohol*, 43 (1), 40-80, 1982 (January).

Lampert, Jean C., *The Human Action of Forgiving: A Critical Application of the Metaphysics of Alfred North Whitehead*, PhD Dissertation, Columbia University, 1980.

Lewis, C. S., *A Grief Observed*, NY: Bantham, 1961.

Martin, J. Arthur, "A Realistic Theory of Forgiveness," in John Wild (ed.), *The Return to Reason*, Chicago: Regnery, 313-332, 1953.

Morris, Herbert, *On Guilt and Innocence*, Berkeley, CA: University of California Press, 1976.

Piaget, Jean, "Problems of Equilibration," in H. Gruber & J. Voneche (eds.), *The Essential Piaget*, NY: Basic Books, 1977.

Measuring Shame:
The Internalized Shame Scale

David R. Cook, EdD

SUMMARY. An experimental scale to measure shame, the Internalized Shame Scale, is described with data on reliability and validity presented from a large nonclinical sample of college students and adults and a small clinical sample that included clients with alcohol problems. Implications from the scale for understanding the phenomenology of shame and its relationship to addictions is discussed.

The phenomenon of shame which has been described in Potter-Efron's article is well-known clinically but has not been studied empirically in any quantitative way. Since the emotion of shame is universally experienced by humans, and since the emotion itself is a necessary aspect of human development, and since we have recognized clinically that "too much" shame can be emotionally crippling, it follows that the frequency and intensity of shame experienced by individuals is quite variable and ought to be measurable. This assumption formed the basis for the development of a scale that would measure the intensity of internalized shame and allow for the study of shame as both a dependent and independent variable.

There are a number of clinical observations regarding shame that have never been tested in any empirical way before and which can be tested with a quantifiable measure of shame. Some of these assumptions are the following: (1) Shame is internalized as a result of experiences of abuse or rejection in one's family of

---

David R. Cook is Professor, Department of Counseling and Psychological Services, University of Wisconsin-Stout.

The author wishes to acknowledge the assistance of Brian Ehrich in writing the original pool of items for the pilot shame scale.

197

origin that evoke the emotion with regular frequency. (2) Shame is associated with significant losses in one's family of origin. (3) Shame is an emotion so painful that it requires defenses that sometimes can take the form of addictive behaviors designed to reduce the pain of the shame. (4) Addictive behaviors can, themselves, contribute to the internalization of shame, as well as being the result of internalized shame.

Based on these assumptions a number of hypotheses regarding shame can be tested. Some hypotheses that particularly bear on the problems of alcoholics and alcohol abusers are the following: (1) Persons addicted to alcohol and/or other drugs will have higher levels of internalized shame than will persons who are not addicted to these substances. (2) Persons with high levels of internalized shame are more likely to be addicted to substances and/or to be multiply addicted than persons with low levels of internalized shame. (3) Persons from families where they experienced significant losses and separations or from families where parents were abusive or rejecting will experience higher levels of internalized shame than will persons who did not suffer losses or grow up in abusive, rejecting families.

If a scale to measure internalized shame is used as a dependent or independent variable in the hypotheses above, and if these hypotheses are supported, then this provides a measure of the validity of the scale. In addition to this, a scale measuring internalized shame makes it possible to examine more closely the phenomenology of shame. And finally, a reliable and valid scale measuring internalized shame can be used as an additional assessment tool in treatment planning and as a clinical tool in both individual and group treatment focusing on problems of internalized shame.

This article describes the development and testing of an internalized shame scale and reports on the reliability and validity of this scale. Implications for use of the scale in assessment and treatment are discussed.

DEVELOPMENT OF SCALE ITEMS

Although descriptions of shame in the psychological literature do not have a long history, there are ample resources that describe the phenomenon, including some that have appeared within the last 10 years (Kaufman, 1985; Lewis, 1971; Lynd, 1958; Tomkins, 1963, Vol. 2; Wurmser, 1981). This literature formed the basis for writing a number of brief statements that would capture as many different facets of the shame experience as possible.

About 90 such statements were written and placed on 3 × 5 cards. These cards were given to a pilot sample of 10 persons who were in inpatient alcoholism treatment and presumed to have high levels of internalized shame. These subjects were asked to sort the cards into two piles, those statements that described experiences or feelings that were familiar and frequent and those that were unfamiliar or happened rarely. Thus, each specific item could be chosen from zero to ten times by the pilot group. An initial selection of items was made for a pilot scale based on those most frequently selected by the ten pilot subjects (Ehrich, 1985).

Items were basically of two types. One type included a number of statements that referred to childhood experiences with parents that were assumed to be shame inducing. The other type of statement directly described an experience or feeling of shame (e.g., I feel like I am never quite good enough). These original items were placed in two separate scales, a childhood scale and an adult scale. There were 23 items in the childhood scale and 48 items on the adult scale. These two scales were administered to about 30 subjects in inpatient alcoholism treatment.

Both scales had high internal reliability. However, the two scales only correlated .58 with each other. The items on the childhood scale did not correlate as highly with the total score as the items on the adult scale. Thus, it was decided to develop a single scale and eliminate most of the childhood scale items. (The Family of Origin Questionnaire, described below, was developed to tap into the childhood shame producing experiences that were eliminated from the shame scale.) A second version of the scale was developed that had 39 items, seven of which were childhood experiences (e.g., My parents belittled me.), and the remainder were statements describing feelings or experiences of shame. These items were selected from the pilot scale on the basis of how well the item correlated with the total score for the 30 pilot subjects and the extent to which any item overlapped or was quite similar to another item.

This 39 item scale was administered to 367 college undergraduates along with a brief survey asking each subject whether or not he/she had been treated for alcoholism, was an abuser of alcohol, was addicted to anything other than alcohol, was the child of an alcoholic parent, had parents who divorced before the subject was 18, had a father who was often absent from the home, had been sexually abused by a family member before age 18, or had lost a parent, sibling, or grandparent by death before age 18. All subjects reporting problems with alcohol, drugs, or other addictions were self-identified and may or may not include subjects who were assessed and treated.

A subgroup of subjects who reported alcohol abuse had a significantly higher mean score on the shame scale than a subgroup who responded "no" to all the survey questions. This version of the shame scale also yielded small but significant correlations with alcohol abuse (.189) and other addictions (.267). Based on these initial data, it appeared that the Internalized Shame Scale was both a reliable and valid measure of the phenomenon of shame (Bauer, 1986).

Reliability and Validity of the Internalized Shame Scale

A third version of the scale was developed following this study to provide a more careful test of the hypotheses listed above. For the third version, all the remaining items referring to childhood experiences with parents were deleted from the scale. A few items were edited for greater clarity. Three new items were written to produce a 35 item scale. The current 35 item version of the Internalized Shame Scale (ISS) has been administered to three different samples at this point. The first sample consisted of 603 undergraduates at a state university in the midwest, including 331 males (55%) and 272 females (45%). The average age was 21 with a range of 18-62. Less than 2% of the sample were nonwhite. The second was an adult sample of 198, including 75 males (38%) and 123 females (62%). The average age of the adult sample was 37.7 with a range of 21-63. This sample was predominantly white. The third sample was a small clinical sample of 64 subjects, 37 from a primary outpatient chemical dependency treatment program, 10 (women) from a refuge for battered women, and 17 subjects under the supervision of a child care protection worker because they had abused or neglected their children. The average age of the clinical group was 27 with a range of 14-51. There were equal number of males and females in the clinical sample.

The internal consistency reliability coefficient for the under-graduate sample was .95. A test-retest correlation of .81 was obtained for 157 undergraduate subjects over intervals ranging from six to eight weeks. Reliability coefficients for the other samples were .95 and .93 indicating substantial internal consistency.

Table 1 shows the means for the ISS for the three samples. One way analysis of variance tests indicated that there was a significant difference between the three groups for the total, $F(2,863) = 16.07$, $p = .0000$; for males, $F(2,435) = 3.95$, $p = .02$; and for females, $F(2,424) = 14.52$, $p = .0000$. A multiple range test (Scheffe procedure) indicated that for the total group and for females the ISS mean for the clinical sample was significantly higher than the means for the undergraduate and adult samples but the latter two did not differ from each other (significance level $= .01$).

Differences between subgroups for males did not reach significance at the .01 level. There were also consistent differences between males and females for all three groups on the ISS with females reporting higher levels of internalized shame than males (Undergraduates, $F(1,601) = 24.55$, $p = .000$; Adults, $F(1,196) = 5.32$, $p = .022$; Clinical, $F(1,62) = 11.93$, $p =$

Table 1

Comparison of ISS means for three samples.

	Total			Males			Females[a]		
	N	M	SD	N	M	SD	N	M	SD
Undergraduate	604	38.5	19.2	331	35.1	17.0	272	42.8	20.7
Adult	198	37.4	20.9	75	33.1	21.3	123	40.1	20.2
Clinical[b]	64	52.8	23.2	32	43.5	17.9	32	62.1	24.4

[a]Female means were significantly higher than males for all groups.

[b]Clinical group mean was significantly higher than other two samples for the total sample and for the female sample.

.001). Further analysis on other variables indicated that in nearly all cases the undergraduate and adult samples did not differ significantly from each other and so they were combined into one large nonclinical sample group for further analyses.

Factor Analysis of Internalized Shame Scale

A factor analysis, using the combined undergraduate and adult sample (N = 801) was carried out in several stages. Based on item analysis statistics seven of the ISS items were considered to be making minimal contribution to the variance of the scale. With these items remaining in the analysis, the varimax rotation produced five factors. When these items were removed a four factor solution accounted for the maximum amount of variance and produced meaningful and reliable factors. Table 2 shows the results of this factor analysis as well as the item statistics for each of the items on the scale. The alpha (internal consistency) reliability coefficients for each factor scale indicate high reliability for the shorter scales.

Validity Tests for Internalized Shame Scale

To test hypotheses that would provide some construct, as well as predictive validity for the ISS, two other measures were completed by the subjects. The Problem History Questionnaire (PHQ) consisted of 24 statements that included 16 different kinds of addictions, two items on partner violence, four on emotional distress, and two items indicating general problems. Subjects responded to each item with a "yes" or a "no," thus providing a self-identified number of addictive behaviors or emotional problems (e.g., anxiety, depression, phobias).

Two major dependent variables were created from the PHQ. The first was the number of addictions reported by subjects and the second was the number of emotional problems. The first was based on the number of yes responses to the 16 items listing addictions. These items included alcohol, illicit drugs, prescription drugs, cigarettes, caffeine, overeating, dieting, bingeing, laxatives, relationship addiction, sex addiction, gambling, running, working, shopping, and shoplifting. Emotional problems included anxiety, depression, suicide threats or attempts, pho-

Table 2

Factor Analysis and Item Statistics[a] for Internalized Shame Scale Items (Full scale alpha= .9534, N= 801)

Items/Factors	Item Mean	Item SD	Item-Tot Corr.	Alpha if Item Del.	Factor Loading
Factor 1: <u>Inadequate and Deficient</u> (Alpha= .9132)					
4. Compared to other people I feel like I somehow never measure up.	1.33	.88	.6543	.9516	.755
7. I see myself as being very small and insignificant.	.98	.88	.6711	.9515	.719
1. I feel like I am never quite good enough.	1.66	.84	.6194	.9519	.706
14. When I compare myself to others I am just not as important.	.96	.88	.6716	.9515	.690
3. I think that people look down on me.	1.18	.74	.5661	.9523	.644
8. I feel intensely inadequate and full of self doubt.	1.03	.90	.7299	.9511	.604
9. I feel as if I am somehow defective as a person, like there is something basically wrong with me.	.74	.87	.7123	.9512	.584
2. I feel somehow left out.	1.62	.82	.5727	.9522	.576
6. I feel insecure about others' opinions of me.	1.69	.95	.6397	.9517	.564
5. I scold myself and put myself down.	1.65	.91	.6354	.9518	.519

TABLE 2 (continued)

Items/Factors	Item Mean	Item SD	Item-Tot Corr.	Alpha if Item Del.	Factor Loading
Factor 2: Embarrassed and Exposed (Alpha=.8421)					
32. When I feel embarrassed I wish I could go back in time and avoid that event.	1.89	1.06	.5478	.9525	.746
31. I could beat myself over the head with a club when I make a mistake.	1.21	.98	.5367	.9525	.649
35. I would like to shrink away when I make a mistake.	1.09	.93	.6122	.9519	.616
24. I seem always to be either watching myself or watching others watch me.	1.30	1.02	.6264	.9518	.570
25. I see myself as striving for perfection only to continually fall short.	1.47	1.06	.6289	.9518	.558
26. I think others are able to see my defects.	1.63	.90	.5929	.9521	.548
10. I have an overpowering fear that my faults will be revealed in front of others.	1.11	.94	.6603	.9516	.432
Factor 3: Fragile and Out of Control (Alpha= .8428)					
21. Sometimes I feel no bigger than a pea.	.52	.70	.5746	.9523	.728
20. I feel as if I have lost control over my body functions and feelings.	.63	.78	.5976	.9521	.698

TABLE 2 (continued)

Items/Factors	Item Mean	Item SD	Item-Tot Corr.	Alpha if Item Del.	Factor Loading
22. At times I feel so exposed that I wish the earth would open up and swallow me.	.54	.78	.6344	.9518	.681
19. At times I feel like I will break into a thousand pieces.	.83	.88	.5878	.9521	.671
23. I become confused when my guilt is overwhelming because I am not sure why I feel guilty.	.92	.91	.6280	.9518	.529
17. I really do not know who I am.	.89	.89	.5863	.9521	.432
Factor 4: Empty and Lonely (Alpha= .8683)					
16. I always feel like there is something missing.	1.20	.98	.6784	.9514	.735
15. My loneliness is more like emptiness.	1.07	1.04	.6785	.9514	.721
11. I have this painful gap within me that I have not been able to fill.	1.03	1.06	.6890	.9513	.703
13. I feel empty and unfulfilled.	1.04	.89	.6840	.9514	.678
18. I replay painful events over and over in my mind until I am overwhelmed.*	1.16	.99	.6004	.9520	.436
Items Deleted from Factor Anal.					
12. There are different parts of me that I try to keep secret from others.	1.61	1.02	.4931	.9529	-
27. When bad things happen to me I feel like I deserve it.	1.26	.93	.4375	.9532	-

TABLE 2 (continued)

Items/Factors	Item Mean	Item SD	Item-Tot Corr.	Alpha if Item Del.	Factor Loading
28. Watching other people feels dangerous to me, like I might be punished for that.	.37	.63	.4605	.9529	-
29. I can't stand to have anyone look directly at me.	.69	.84	.5192	.9526	-
30. It is difficult for me to accept a compliment.	1.40	1.07	.4808	.9531	-
33. Suffering, degradation and distress seems to fascinate and excite me.	.31	.63	.3901	.9533	-
34. I feel dirty and messy and feel like no one should ever touch me or they'll be dirty too.	.16	.42	.4253	.9532	-

*Alpha for factor if this item deleted= .8845

[a]All item statistics are based on the full 35 item scale.

bias, hospitalization for three or more days, and a perception of one's self as having "lots of problems." The violence items were not included in this analysis.

The second of the two additional measures, the Family of Origin Questionnaire (FOQ), consisted of nine items asking about losses and separations before subjects were 18 and another 24 items asking about experiences with mother and father separately of abuse, rejection, abandonment, parental alcoholism and parental conflict while growing up. This instrument yielded both a total score, taken as a measure of family dysfunction, and several subscale scores based on logically related items. These subscale scores included the following: parental alcoholism, parental physical and sexual abuse, threats of abandonment, mother rejection, father rejection, parental conflict, and "no talk rule" in the family.

The subscale scores for the FOQ, the number of losses and separations, and the factor scores for the ISS were entered into a multiple regression correlation as predictor variables with number of addictions and number of emotional problems as the dependent variables. A significance level of .01 was selected as the criterion for a predictor variable to remain in the equation. The shame factors, separations, and losses were entered first to maximize their contribution to the predicted variance and the family of origin subscales were entered last so that whatever additional variance they predicted would not be the result of the correlation of family of origin variables with shame. These correlations were carried out first for the total nonclinical sample and total clinical samples, and then for the nonclinical sample of males and females separately. Since the clinical sample was rather small, separate analyses of males and females was not carried out. Table 3A & B shows the results of the regression equations for the two samples.

An inspection of Table 3A & B shows that of the four shame scale factors, the sense of feeling fragile and out of control and empty and lonely were the most potent predictors of both number of addictions and number of problems for the nonclinical sample, accounting for about 13% of the variance in number of addictions and almost 27% of the variance in number of emotional problems. Both separations and losses account for a statistically significant increase in the predicted variance of addictions, but not of emotional problems. The family of origin issues that emerged as most predictive of addictions were parental abuse, no talk rule, and threats of abandonment, accounting for about another 5% of the variance, a statistically significant increase. For emotional problems, rejection by mother and father, parental abuse, and parental alcoholism all entered the equation adding an additional 7% of predicted variance.

For the clinical sample, only the shame factor of "fragile and out of control" remained in the equation, but it accounted for almost 15% of the variance in addictions and 51% of the variance in emotional problems, clearly indicating the importance of these internalized feelings in maintaining addictions and emotional distress. Losses added a significant increase in the predicted variance of addictions for the clinical group. Only one family of origin factor emerged as a significant predictor for the clinical group for each of the dependent variables. For number of addictions, parental conflict added 10% to the predicted variance. For number of emotional problems, mother rejection added about another 5% of predicted variance.

Table 4A & B shows the multiple regression equations for the males and females in the nonclinical sample. Age was added as a variable and entered first in each equation, followed by the

TABLE 3A

Hierarchical Multiple Regression Equations with ISS Factor Scores

and Family of Origin Subscale Scores (stepwise entry for ISS factors

and FOS subscales)

Non-Clinical Sample: N=801

CRITERION	PREDICTOR	R	R²	r	Fª	Beta
Number of	ISS 3	.344	.119	.344	107.52	.2129***
Addictions	ISS 4	.360	.129	.317	59.54	.0999*
	Separations	.380	.145	.170	44.99	.0665*
	Losses	.391	.153	.139	35.85	.0813*
	PARAB	.419	.176	.215	33.99	.1114**
	NOTALK	.438	.192	.224	31.37	.1230***
	ABAND	.445	.198	.214	28.05	.0898**
Number of	ISS 4	.485	.235	.485	245.87	.2308***
Emotional	ISS 3	.519	.269	.473	147.28	.2419***
Problems	Separations	.527	.278	.160	102.29	-.0069
	Losses	.527	.278	.074	76.68	4.051
	MOREJ	.566	.320	.330	74.93	.1762***
	FAREJ	.581	.337	.311	57.39	.0970**
	PARAB	.588	.346	.234	59.86	.0968**
	PARALC	.593	.352	.188	53.70	.0818**

TABLE 3B

Clinical Sample: N=63

CRITERION	PREDICTOR	R	R^2	r	F^a	Beta
Number of	ISS 3	.383	.147	.383	10.65	.2991**
Addictions	Separations	.404	.163	.163	5.94	-.1104
	Losses	.472	.223	.349	5.74	.2988**
	PARCON	.567	.322	.351	6.99	.3436**
Number of	ISS 3	.717	.514	.717	65.62	.6447***
Emotional	Separations	.726	.527	.181	34.02	.0108
Problems	Losses	.729	.532	.255	22.77	.0382
	MOREJ	.765	.584	.431	20.75	.2561**

ISS 3=Fragile and Out of Control   ISS 4=Empty and Lonely

PARAB=Physical & sexual abuse from mother and/or father

NOTALK=Family observed "no talk rule"

ABAND=Parental threats of abandonment, including suicide threats

MOREJ=Rejecting mother   FAREJ=Rejecting father

PARALC=Parental alcoholism   PARCON=Parental conflict, incl. battering

^{a}All F values significant at <.004

t value for Beta significant at <.05* <.01** <.001***

shame factors, losses, separations, and the family of origin sub-scales.

The correlations in Table 4A & B indicate the importance of the same two shame factors for both males and females, although only "fragile and out of control" remained in the equation for males predicting number of addictions. Separations was a significant predictor of addictions for males, but did not contribute significantly to emotional problems. Neither losses nor separations entered into the equation for females. On family of origin variables, there were clear differences between the males and females. The no talk rule and parental abuse added another 6% of the predicted variance of addictions for males. Only the mother rejection subscale contributed to the prediction of addictions for females, adding about 3% more predicted variance. For males, threats of abandonment, parental alcoholism, and parental abuse all contribute to the number of emotional problems. For females both mother rejection and father rejection contribute to emotional problems.

DISCUSSION

Several observations can be made from the data presented here. First, with regard to internalized shame, it would appear

TABLE 4A

Hierarchical multiple regression equations entering age, ISS factors, separations losses, family of origin subscales for total non-clinical sample by males and females.

				MALES (N=406)		
CRITERION	PREDICTOR	R	R^2	r	F^a	Beta
Number of	Age	.021	.000	.021	0.19ns	.0275
Addictions	ISS 3	.348	.121	.341	27.76	.2848***
	Separations	.377	.142	.187	22.20	.1094*
	NOTALK	.419	.176	.242	21.46	.1634***
	PARAB	.446	.199	.261	19.91	.1589***
Number of	Age	.036	.001	.036	0.53ns	.0835
Emotional	ISS 3	.494	.244	.483	64.92	.2656***
Problems	ISS 4	.534	.286	.474	53.60	.2295***
	Separations	.552	.305	.197	43.99	.0444
	ABAND	.587	.344	.340	42.06	.1608***
	PARALC	.607	.368	.264	38.76	.1515***
	PARAB	.617	.381	.289	35.05	.1240**

TABLE 4B

CRITERION	PREDICTOR	R	R^2	r	F^a	Beta
				FEMALES (N=393)		
Number of	Age	.000	.000	----	.00ns	.0263
Addictions	ISS 3	.399	.159		36.97	.2561***
	ISS 4	.418	.175		27.51	.1522*
	MOREJ	.455	.207		25.43	.1884***
Number of	Age	.114	.013		5.15*	.1301**
Emotional	ISS 4	.496	.246		63.86	.2083***
Problems	ISS 3	.527	.278		50.12	.2578***
	MOREJ	.570	.325		46.84	.1916***
	FAREJ	.590	.348		41.44	.1621***

[a]All F values significant at <.001 (unless otherwise noted)

t value for Beta significant at <.05* <.01** <.001***

Order of entry for predictor variables: 1) age (forced); 2) ISS factors;

3) losses, separations; 4) FOS subscales

ISS 3=Fragile and Out of Control   ISS 4=Empty and Lonely

PARAB=Physical & sexual abuse from mother and/or father

NOTALK=Family observed "no talk rule"

ABAND=Parental threats of abandonment, including suicide threats

MOREJ=Rejecting mother   FAREJ=Rejecting father

PARALC=Parental alcoholism

that the phenomenon of shame is not a single factor but consists of different kinds of internalized feelings, some of which are more painful and dysfunctional than others. The factors labeled "fragile and out of control" and "empty and lonely" appear to be the most potent contributors to the development and/or the maintenance of problems of addiction and emotional distress for both clinical and nonclinical groups. The ISS also appears to account for more of the variance of emotional problems than of addictions. In general, all predictor variables accounted for more of the variance in number of emotional problems than number of addictions. Since addictions are, in large part, habitual patterns of behavior in which learning plays an important part, there are perhaps many other situational factors that enter into the development of an addictive behavior than is the case for emotional problems. Shame, losses, separations, and family dysfunction can thus account more directly for the development of emotional problems.

It is clear that family dysfunction does play an important part in the development of addictions and emotional problems. Parental abuse of children, especially males, creates great vulnerability for later addictions. Although the present clinical sample is small, there is an indication that for more severe levels of addictions, parental conflict plays a significant part, along with feelings of fragility and being "out of control."

IMPLICATIONS FOR TREATING ALCOHOLISM

Facing Shame: Families in Recovery

A recent book by Fossum and Mason (1986) provides the most thorough clinical exploration of shame and its relationship to addictions that is currently available. They note that "one of the most clearly identifiable aspects of shame in families is addictive behavior. The addiction becomes a central organizing principle for the system, maintaining the system as well as its shame" (Fossum & Mason, 1986, p.123). They also point out that "while many families have successfully completed treatment programs for chemical dependency or anorexia nervosa or bulimia, these control-oriented, shame-bound systems retain their addictive dynamics. Families at the high end of the continuum of shame often manifest multiple addictions. It is not uncommon to see compulsive drug use accompanied by compulsive overeating or starving or work habits in one or more family members" (p.124). The data reported here provides direct support for this clinical observation. *For both males and females, the higher the levels of shame the greater the number of addictions/problems.*

Internalized shame leaves the individual vulnerable to becoming addicted to an experience such as drinking or using mood altering drugs. At the same time such addictive use of alcohol or drugs serves to deepen and maintain the shame-based identity. Disrupting the addictive pattern is crucial to breaking the cycle of maintained shame, but does not in itself heal the shame-bound individual. At the same time, identifying the internalized shame and its roots in the family system can be an important aspect of treatment that is aimed at disrupting or terminating the addictive behavior.

Although the Internalized Shame Scale is still in an experimental stage of development and more appropriate for research than clinical use at this time, these early results strongly support its validity as a measure of shame and substantiate the important relationship between high levels of shame and addictive behavior. Alcoholism treatment professionals should be prepared to recognize the presence of shame-based identities in all their patients, to identify other addictive patterns besides alcoholism that will almost certainly be present, and to find ways to help patients begin to recognize their painful feelings as the shame that they internalized from experiences growing up in their families.

Hopefully, in the near future, the Internalized Shame Scale (see Table 5) will provide a useful tool for this process of identification and exploration of internalized shame experiences for addicted individuals and their families. Knowing something about the intensity of shame that has been internalized by the alcoholic patient can help sensitize the treatment professional to the likelihood of strong defensive reactivity to such basic expectations in treatment as acknowledging one's loss of control over one's behavior, a very shame inducing admission. Pushing a patient too hard, too early for such an acknowledgement (e.g., acceptance of step one of AA) may only intensify the feelings of shame and the necessary defense of denial. But if the shame is identified and labeled (for example, by taking and discussing the results of the ISS), the patient can be helped to see how his/her addictive pattern serves to maintain the shame and therefore how it is that breaking the addictive cycle can help break the painful cycle of shame as well.

TABLE 5
INTERNALIZED SHAME SCALE

Copyright 1986 by David R.Cook

DIRECTIONS: Below is a list of statements describing feelings or experiences that you may have from time to time or that are familiar to you because you have had these feelings and experiences for a long time. These are all statements of feelings and experiences that are generally painful or negative in some way. Some people will seldom or never have had many of these feelings and experiences. Everyone has had some of these feelings at some time, but if you find that these statements describe the way you feel a good deal of the time, it can be painful just reading them. Try to be as honest as you can in responding.

Read each statement carefully and mark the number in the space to the left of the item that indicates the frequency with which you find yourself feeling or experiencing what is described in the statement. Use the scale below. DO NOT OMIT ANY ITEM.

SCALE

NEVER- 0	SELDOM- 1	SOMETIMES- 2	FREQUENTLY- 3	ALMOST ALWAYS- 4

_____1. I feel like I am never quite good enough.

_____2. I feel somehow left out.

_____3. I think that people look down on me.

_____4. Compared to other people I feel like I somehow never measure up.

_____5. I scold myself and put myself down.

_____6   I feel insecure about others' opinions of me.

_____7. I see myself as being very small and insignificant.

_____8. I feel intensely inadequate and full of self doubt.

_____9. I feel as if I am somehow defective as a person, like there is something basically wrong with me.

_____10. I have an overpowering fear that my faults will be revealed in front of others.

_____11. I have this painful gap within me that I have not been able to fill.

_____12. There are different parts of me that I try to keep secret from others.

_____13. I feel empty and unfulfilled.

_____14. When I compare myself to others I am just not as important.

_____15. My loneliness is more like emptiness.

_____16. I always feel like there is something missing

_____17. I really do not know who I am.

_____18. I replay painful events over and over in my mind until I feel overwhelmed.

_____19. At times I feel like I will break into a thousand pieces.

_____20. I feel as if I have lost control over my body functions and my feelings.

_____21. Sometimes I feel no bigger than a pea.

_____22. At times I feel so exposed that I wish the earth would open up and swallow me.

TABLE 5 (continued)

SCALE

NEVER- 0	SELDOM- 1	SOMETIMES- 2	FREQUENTLY- 3	ALMOST ALWAYS- 4

____23. I become confused when my guilt is overwhelming because I am not sure why I feel guilty.

____24. I seem always to be either watching myself or watching others watch me.

____25. I see myself striving for perfection only to continually fall short.

____26. I think others are able to see my defects.

____27. When bad things happen to me I feel like I deserve it.

____28. Watching other people feels dangerous to me, like I might be punished for that.

____29. I can't stand to have anyone look directly at me.

____30. It is difficult for me to accept a compliment.

____31. I could beat myself over the head with a club when I make a mistake.

____32. When I feel embarrassed, I wish I could go back in time and avoid that event.

____33. Suffering Degradation and distress seems to fascinate and excite me.

____34. I feel dirty and messy like no one should ever touch me or they'll be dirty too.

____35. I would like to shrink away when I make a mistake.

REFERENCES

Bauer, D. R., (1986). *Investigation of shame as reported by a college population on the s-scale*, (Unpublished Masters Thesis, University of Wisconsin-Stout), Menomonie, WI.

Ehrich, B. J., (1985). *The development and pilot testing of a shame scale* (Unpublished Masters Thesis, University of Wisconsin-Stout).

Fossum, M. A. & Mason, M. J., (1986). *Facing shame: Families in recovery*, New York: W. W. Norton.

Kaufman, G., (1985). *Shame: The power of caring* (rev. ed.), Cambridge, MA: Schenkman.

Lewis, H. B., (1971). *Shame and guilt in neurosis*, New York: International University.

Lynd, H. M., (1958). *On shame and the search for identity*, New York: Harcourt Brace.

Tomkins, S. S., (1963). *Affect, imagery, and consciousness*, New York: Springer.

Wurmser, L., (1981). *The mask of shame*, Baltimore: Johns Hopkins University Press.

Index